AF291773

Silicon Fen

Edited by Simon Willmoth and Steven Bode
Published by Film and Video Umbrella
www.silicon-fen.org.uk

Silicon Fen

Suky Best
Susan Collins
Dalziel + Scullion
Annabel Howland
Stephen Hughes
TNWK

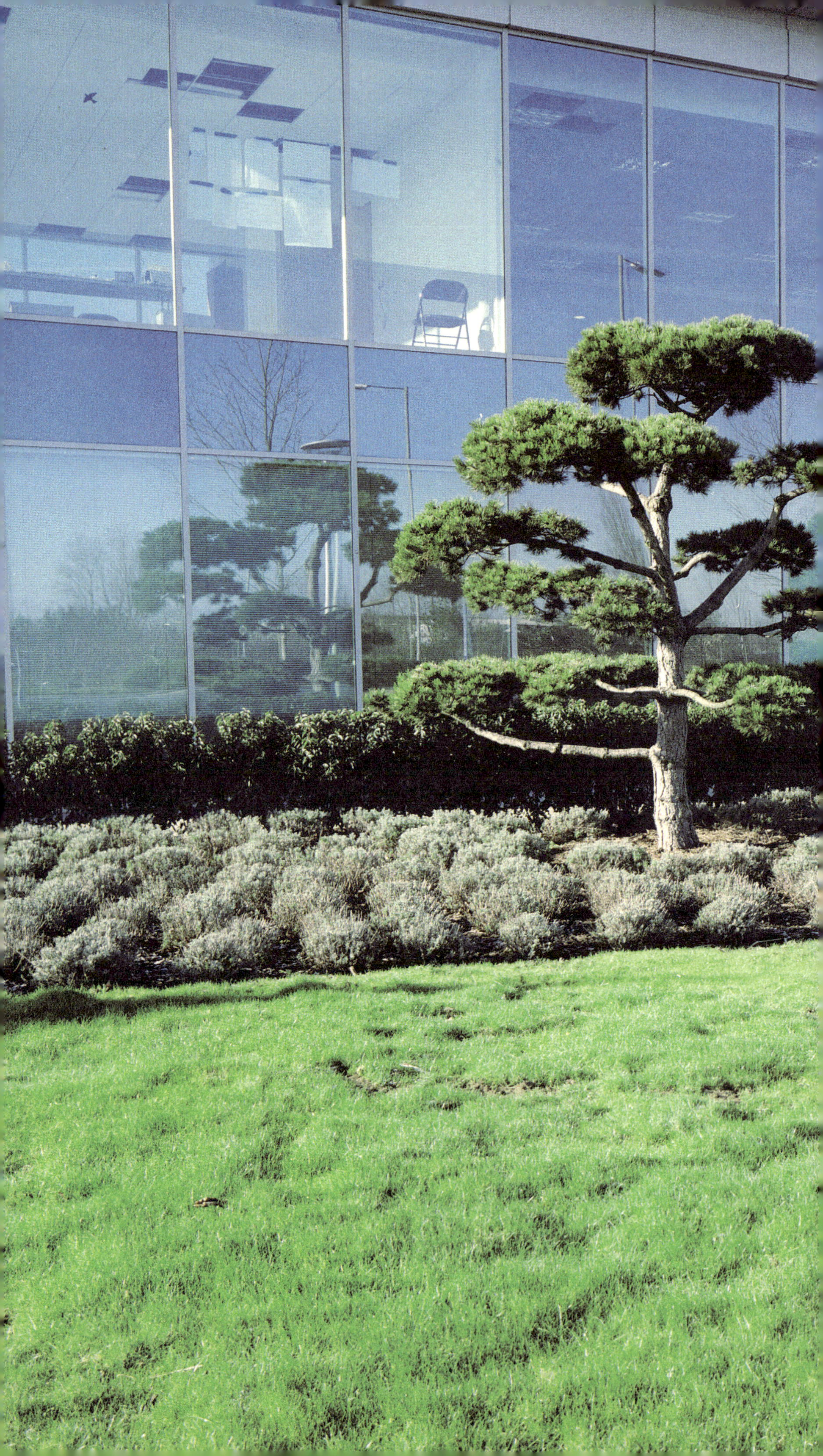

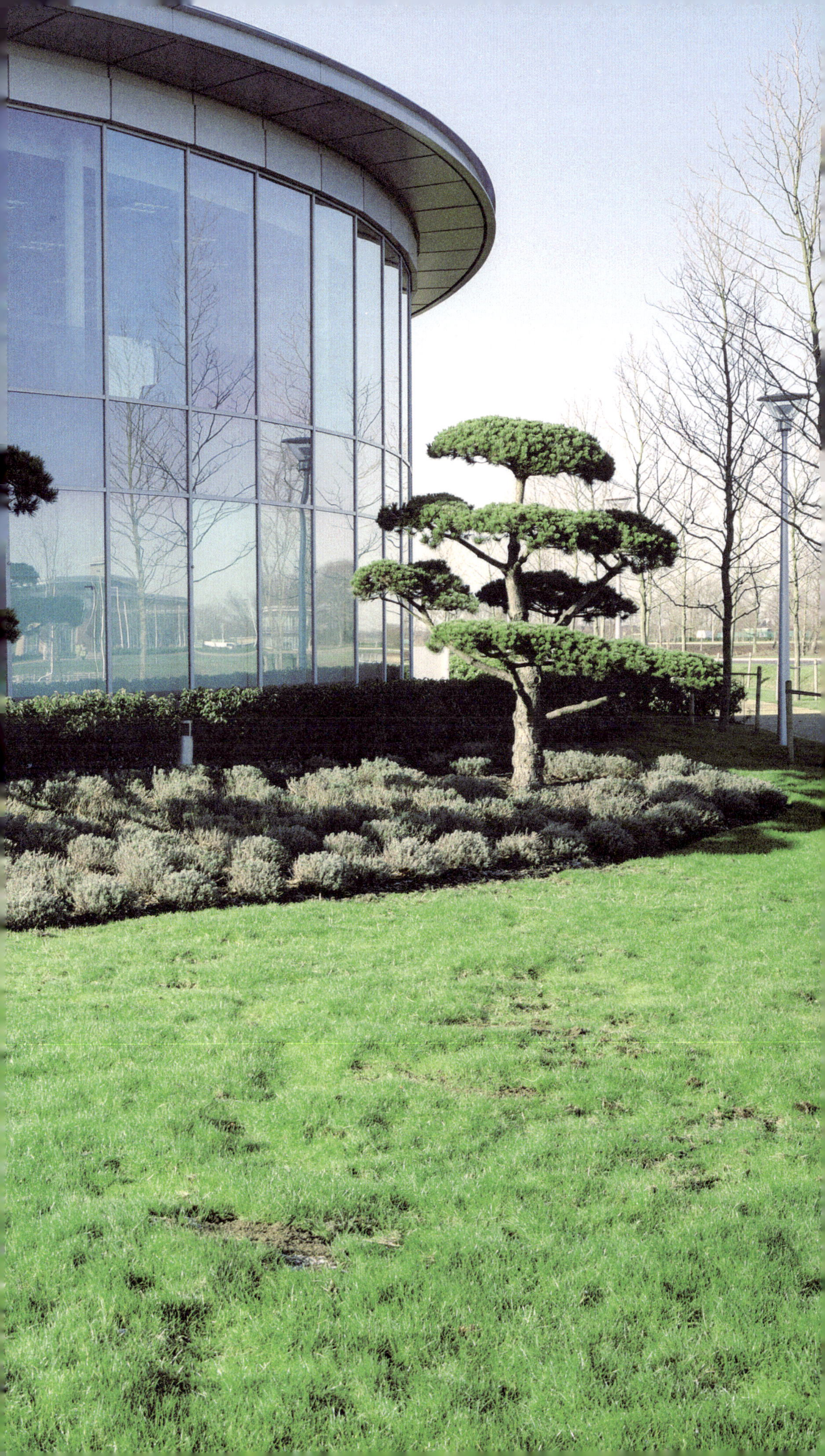

Contents

Foreword Iain Sinclair

*'They pass over here in boats into the fenn-country, and over
the famous washes into Lincolnshire, but the passage is very
dangerous and uneasy, and where passengers often miscarry
and are lost.'*

Daniel Defoe, *A Tour Through the Whole Island of Great Britain*

Walking, through three shimmering summer days, in the traces of
John Clare, from Epping Forest to Glinton, I discovered a new England:
agribiz acres, waist-high cereal fields, tough weeds breaking up
abandoned airstrips, commuter villages with no obvious signs of life.
And budget versions of the Millennium Dome peddling McTimoney
Chiropractic therapies on the outskirts of towns that were all outskirt
and no centre. Notional settlements built to be avoided, ring roads
as amnesiac boulevards: fine until you get out of the car. The ruins
of filling stations, the fast-food franchises given over to China Moon
with its motel facilities and guardian lions. Pulling away from the
gravitational clot of London, we learn to negotiate invisible boundaries
between recently colonised off-highway zones and empty quarters
that nobody has yet found a way to exploit. Limestone outcrops yield
to black fens, alluvia. It did for Clare, more than the enclosures, more
than the bitter drag of poverty and the hurt of language, this shift of
a couple of miles from his home place, Helpston, to Northborough,
right on the edge of that watery horror: the flatlands, the levels, habitat of demons.

Now reality-defying settlements like Cambourne appear overnight,
you can hear them unroll the bubblewrap. Guard dogs slaver at the
gates of deserted farms. Mechanical voices warn off intruders.
Surveillance cameras swivel on perimeter fences. When I found the
remote Fenland farm where my wife's family once kept pigs and serviced
thirsty watermen, the house was occupied by a Chinese entrepreneur
who had been prosecuted for allowing the ducks he was fattening to
starve, their food devoured by rats who gnawed their way through
the ancient barn door.

Highway planners labour to protect us from manifestations of that awful nullity, the resurrected jigsaw of England's oriental margin with its collaged rectangles, pylons, corrugated swine-bivouacs and wind-breaking tree clumps. We motor through green passages, strategically planted banks and verges, seeing nothing beyond the play of reflections on dirty windscreens. We are protected from particulars of place, the magnum cinema of waterland skies. In this reverie of the road, we might as well be crawling down the tunnel of a crop-forcing poly-thene-skinned hoop. Which is why the activities of sponsored witnesses, artists as agents, is so significant. And necessary. With their covert technologies, the tacit acknowledgement of the cost of economic adventurism, they are, at once, descendants of the surveyors Clare discovered out in the fields, plotting the East Coast railway, and of the poet himself: a maker of songs voyaging into madness. The more you know, the greater the pain. Wild nature is all too eager to forget us, to break off this unequal alliance.

Commissioned artists, venturing into a conceptual nowhere, are tolerated as a kind of low-level acoustic interference, a steady-state hum, ghosts of the future. They are absorbed into the long social history of struggle, subsistence living, civil wars, night raids and unlisted human cargoes. There is an ethical boundary between places that are bombed, industrial cities, docks, power plants, and the nuclear silos and airstrips from which death-delivering monsters take off. The pre-silicon fen, only accessible by water, was ditched and drained: the better to be milked. As a virus-incubating fowl-pest colony. A nest of wind farms. Superstores. Science parks built by robots as digital photo-opportunities. Sponsored outsiders, hearts on sleeves, make new work to celebrate difference. Open-field artists, like ants or cockroaches, will be the final colonists. Trained to catalogue and provoke, they accept this challenge: forge vision out of moral bankruptcy, political short-termism, clouds of unknowing. *Silicon Fen* is an honourable account of what can and cannot be achieved in a place that, as soon as it is described, will no longer be there.

This publication is, first and foremost, a record of an innovative visual arts project that developed a series of exhibitions of new artwork at venues across the East of England between 2004 and 2007. A consideration of how landscape in general, and the East Anglian landscape in particular, has been both affected and reflected by technology, *Silicon Fen* brought together a number of still and moving-image works by artists whose facility with digital forms of image-making conjured up a clearer and more detailed picture of a part of the country whose traditional place on the geographical margins belies its increasingly influential position at the leading edge of recent technological advances.

A collaboration between Norwich University College of the Arts (formerly Norwich School of Art and Design) and Film and Video Umbrella, the initiative was extended through a series of co-commissioning and exhibition partnerships with galleries in the region, all of which were located within, or within striking distance of, the Fens. Immersing themselves in the distinctive history and topography of the Fenlands, the participating artists (Suky Best, Susan Collins, Dalziel + Scullion, Annabel Howland, Stephen Hughes and TNWK) contributed a series of online, wall-based or installation pieces that deftly capture the spirit of this deceptively remote landscape and help to illuminate its disarmingly complex nature.

Silicon Fen commissioned artists from the locality, already familiar with its singular environment, as well as artists from outside the region discovering it for the first time, including an artist from Holland highlighting affinities and parallels between the two countries. Each of the artists offered new and unexpected insights into a landscape whose surface features often belie its considerable underlying interest. Much more than a meditation on 'place' (or that contemporary phenomenon, the 'non-place'), the works also acted as a barometer of change, their focus on media networks and technological formations echoing recent infrastructural developments across the region, as well as providing a perceptual framework through which the surrounding landscape, and the recurring patterns that can be traced within it,

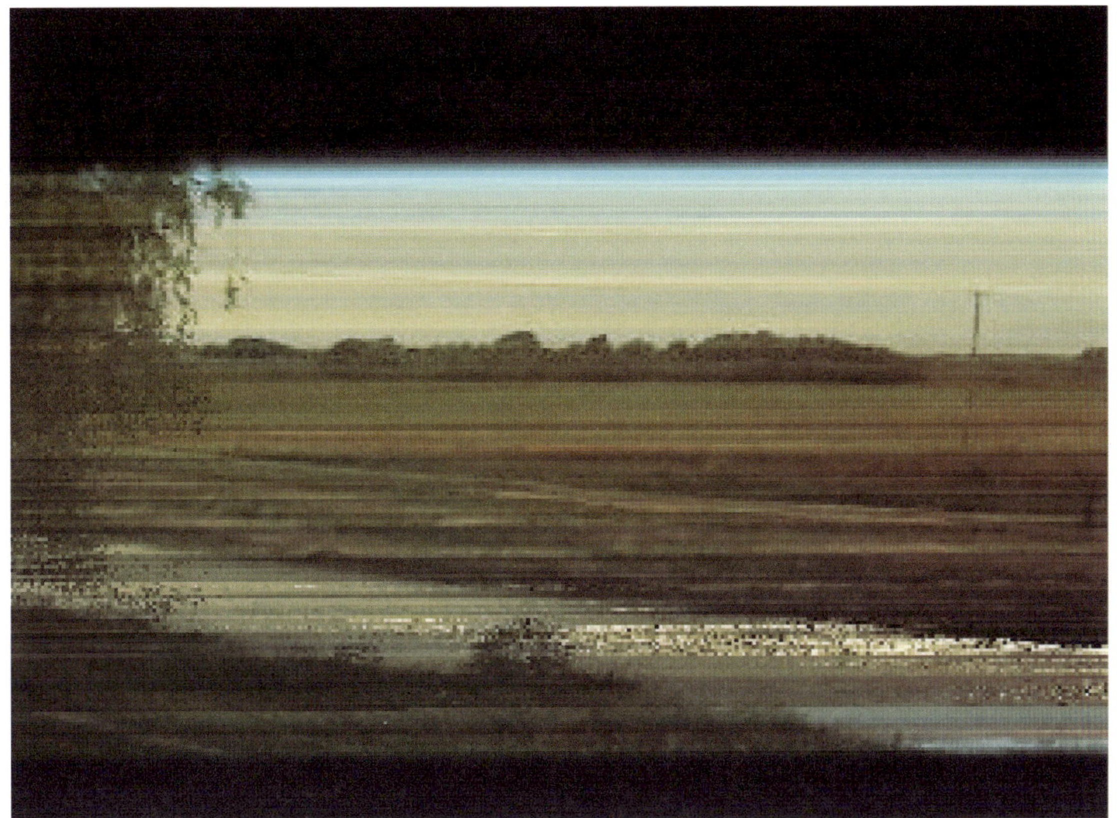

might be better understood.

Alongside documentation and descriptions of the commissioned works, this publication further profiles the featured artists through interviews and other contextualising material. Broadening out from this immediate focus on the individual artists' pieces, it also assembles a number of imaginative and informative texts that prompt wider reflection on the geography and history of the Fens, and the future that is being mapped out in and around them. Our thanks go to all the artists involved for their energy, invention and commitment to the project, to the venues in Bedford, Ely, King's Lynn and Peterborough for their contribution to both the development and staging of the commissions, and, finally, to the various funding bodies, particularly Arts Council England East and the Mondriaan Foundation, without whose support *Silicon Fen* would not have been possible.

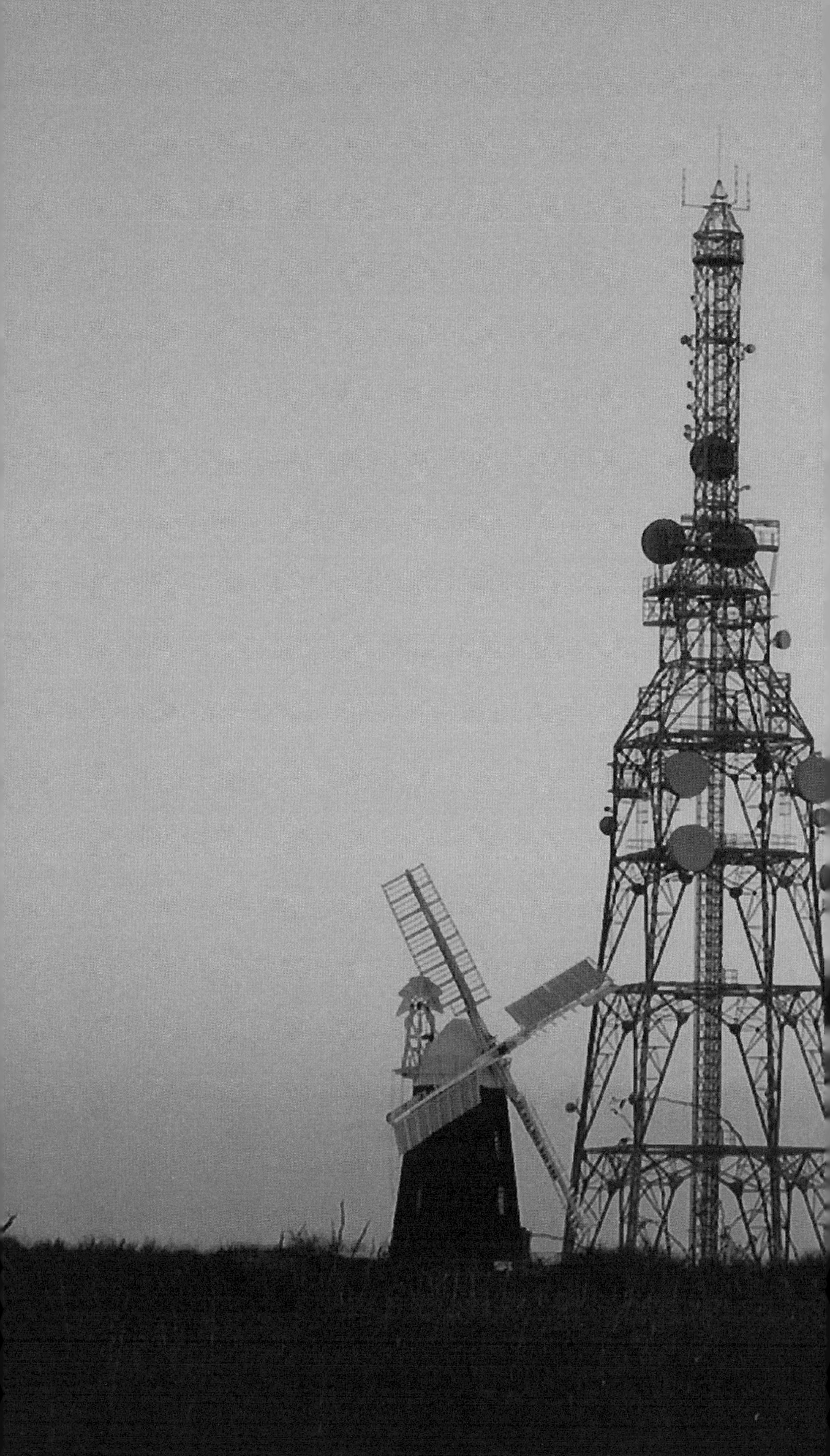

A cloud has formed over most of Norwich, stretching away to the southwest in the direction of Cambridge. Closely packed above the centre of the city, it gets more patchy as it reaches the open country, as if its presence was partly dependent on the extent of human activity beneath it. There is an element of truth in all this, of course; not that anyone is in a hurry to mention it — should they ever speak of the cloud at all. An item of conversation when it first appeared, it has faded from people's immediate consciousness to become just another background feature in the ever-growing hubbub of contemporary life. Further out, over the flatlands of the Fens, the cloud disperses, unable to gain a purchase, its break-up into isolated pockets finding an echo in the lie of the land below, where solitary farms and scattered hamlets stand out like dots in an otherwise empty and featureless terrain. Everything is quiet; nonetheless, you sense a change is in the air. It may not have made it here just yet, but the day the cloud becomes fully established cannot be too far away.

The cloud in question is not a meteorological phenomenon but a recent technological innovation, a blanket of continuous wireless coverage that has been rolled out across the city and that only ceases beyond its borders. Sitting in one of Norwich's many wi-fi enabled cafés, with the bells of St Andrew's and St Swithin's cascading around me, I am reminded, once again, how history, in apparently ringing the changes, so often repeats itself. Where Norwich was previously noted for the number of its churches (more than any equivalent city in Northern Europe), it is now equally extravagantly blessed with a plethora of wi-fi hotspots, each of them thrumming in invisible communion; under whose beneficent dispensation users of computers or handheld devices can go online, at no cost, at any place and at any moment.

The Cloud (to give it is correct industry appellation) is, indeed, a miracle, of sorts; a latterday marvel whose weightless all-enabling omnipresence offers an almost perfect expression of the modern technological *zeitgeist*. It also figures just as prominently on any barometer of future trends. Though barely more than a little ripple in the ether, it is as much of a portent as any band of cirrus or cumulonimbus; a sign, furthermore, that if technology is not already making the wider cultural weather, it is, more and more, the medium through which we read it. And, like any new and prevailing system, it suggests ways in which people might best equip themselves for the times ahead. Although similar wireless clouds have been propagated in financial hubs such as the City of London, Norwich (along with other like-minded, and more obviously future-oriented urban centres such as Milton Keynes) has invested heavily in a digital communications infrastructure with the potential to connect, and inform, a wider cross-section of its citizens, trusting that a switched-on, media-literate population will give it an edge in the knowledge economy of the future.

The emergence of Norwich as one of Britain's first wireless cities is only the latest in a series of eye-catching initiatives emanating from the East of England, a part of the country once thought of as detached and remote, but now increasingly at the forefront of new technological advances. A prime mover in this remarkable *Vorsprung durch Technik* is the presence of Cambridge University, a longstanding centre of excellence in science and technology whose culture of innovation sparked the growth of numerous offshoot companies, who have since become leaders in the fields of electronics, software development and biotechnology. Set up in the shadow of their *alma mater*, and benefiting from a continually replenishing talent pool and burgeoning inward investment, this constellation of trailblazing firms, grouped together in what became known as the 'Cambridge Cluster', was quickly adopted by commentators eager to broker comparisons with California's booming Silicon Valley. Following the convention in which prospective members of this exclusive hi-tech club would be badged with both a gleaming silicon marque and according to their main topographical feature (Berkshire's imitation Silicon Valley; Scotland's short-lived Silicon Glen), it was no surprise that, when the techno parks and research campuses started expanding from the outskirts of Cambridge into the surrounding landscape, the area gained its own new-fangled moniker: Silicon Fen.

Not all claims along this new technological frontier have been put down in out-of-the-way or otherwise untapped locations. New York's Silicon Alley, for example, evokes a very different, unequivocally urban frontline: crowded and alpha-competitive, though frequently equally 'out-there' in its pursuit of future pay dirt; panhandling for a flash of a killer idea among the clamour and crush of the city. Usually, however, these new-tech developments are founded, and explicitly rooted, in both an actual and a rhetorical proximity to nature: as if a virgin, or at very least verdant, backdrop was a *sine qua non* of any pioneering business, or a greenfield site a prerequisite of blue sky thinking. In this way, a number of myths are perpetuated: not least of which is the myth of the frontier itself, its can-do spirit and Utopian origins belying a more fundamental tension in man's relationship to nature that persists across much of the developed

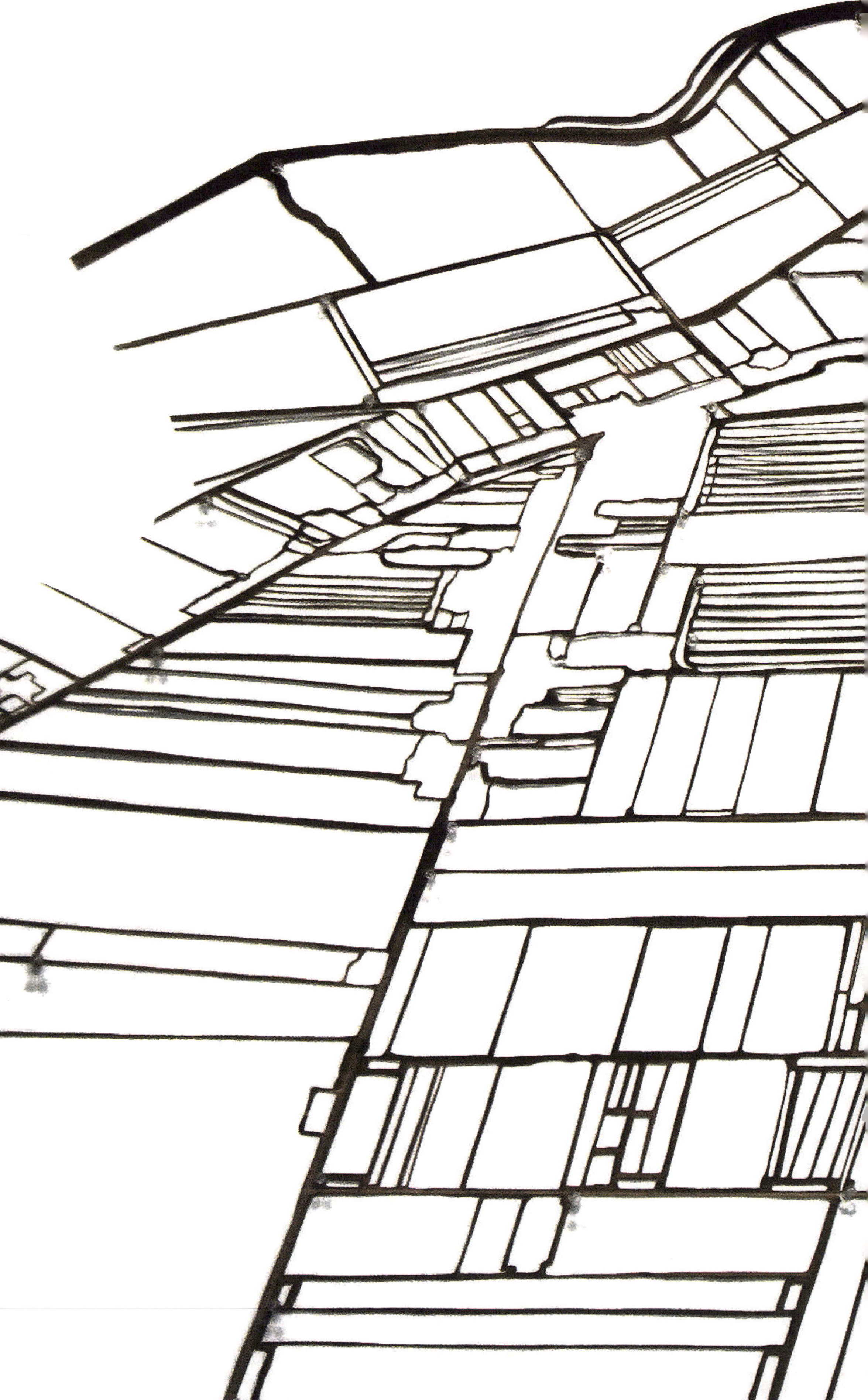

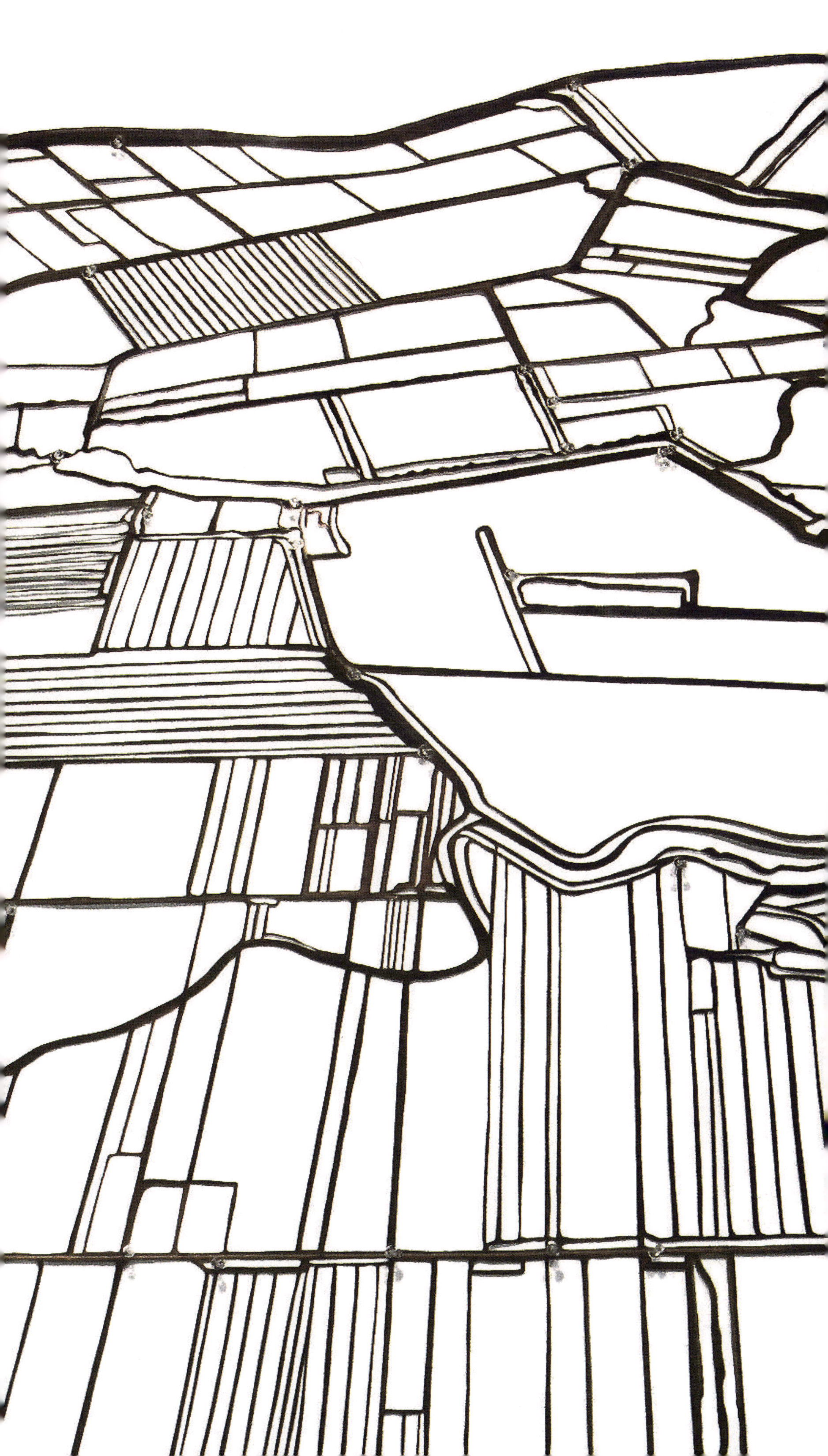

world; between a desire to be at one with nature, and an urge to subdue it, or supplant it.

The featureless, sometimes desolate vistas of East Anglia are unlikely ever to be mistaken for either a remnant of Eden or a glimpse of Arcadia. Although large parts of the landscape are still disarmingly green, much is the preserve of prolific and rapacious agribusiness, its endless polytunnels glinting in the light alongside vestigial ribbons of drainage ditches. Away from these vast, multi-acre plots, ground that has been set aside or not considered for cultivation takes on an even more marginal aspect; not wild exactly, but well off the beaten path, curiously voided of interest. Or, perhaps, it is the sheer unalleviated flatness of this part of the world that gives it the appearance of a *tabula rasa*, one that almost demands that man mark it with traces of his presence, if only to ameliorate its stultifying drabness. Certainly, the monotonous blankness of whatever open ground still remains acts almost as an open invitation to planners and developers to speed the arrival of new business, or, with an equal lack of protest, to put up more houses.

The East Anglian Fenlands may seem like a rural backwater, bypassed by much of recent history, but they are, and have been for many generations, a profoundly man-made landscape. As the latest wave of start-up companies spreads out from Cambridge to Ely and beyond, their futuristic, slightly alien buildings standing out sharply against the empty horizon, they encounter the edge of a much greater landmark that was the engineering phenomenon of its day — the network of canals, sluices and run-off ditches, built by the Dutch architect Cornelius Vermuyden in the 17th century, to drain this low-lying, perennially inundated basin for agricultural exploitation. Designed to regulate the flow of water (in ways that echo our contemporary preoccupation with optimising the circulation of information), Vermuyden's audaciously state-of-the-art *grand projet* offers an intriguing analogue for the intricate web of communications infrastructure that is starting to fan out across this part of the country. An interesting precursor of what we might now call a distributed network, these Fenland canals brim with other historical parallels — originally constructed as part of a wider strategic alliance between the British and the Dutch (one that prefigures the ever-closer

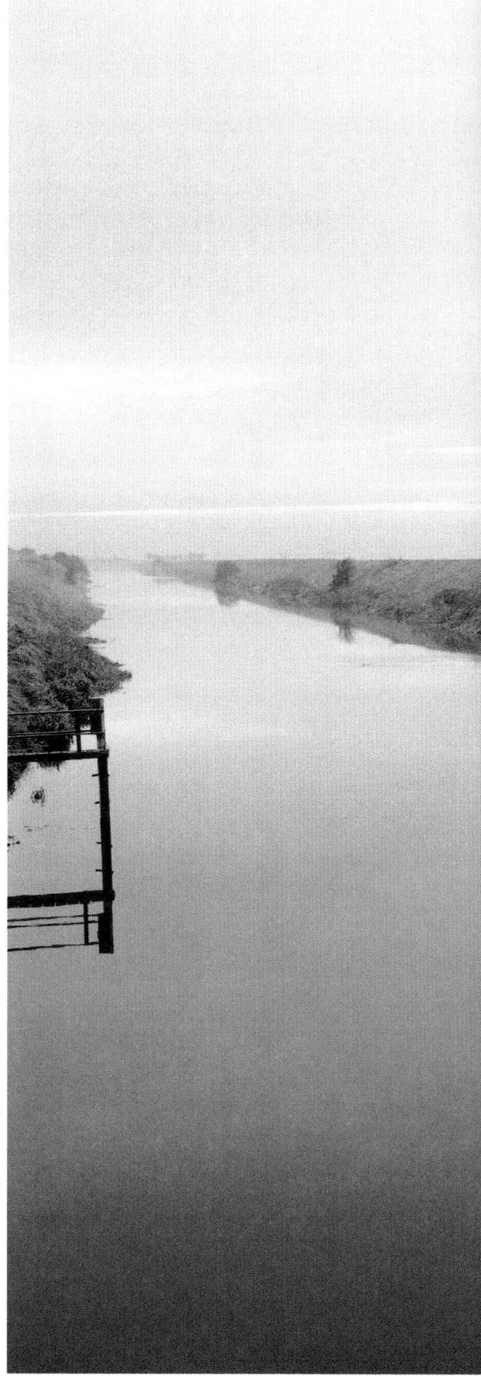

Previous page – Annabel Howland *Drains, Cables, and Cuts*
This page – Stephen Hughes *Untitled*

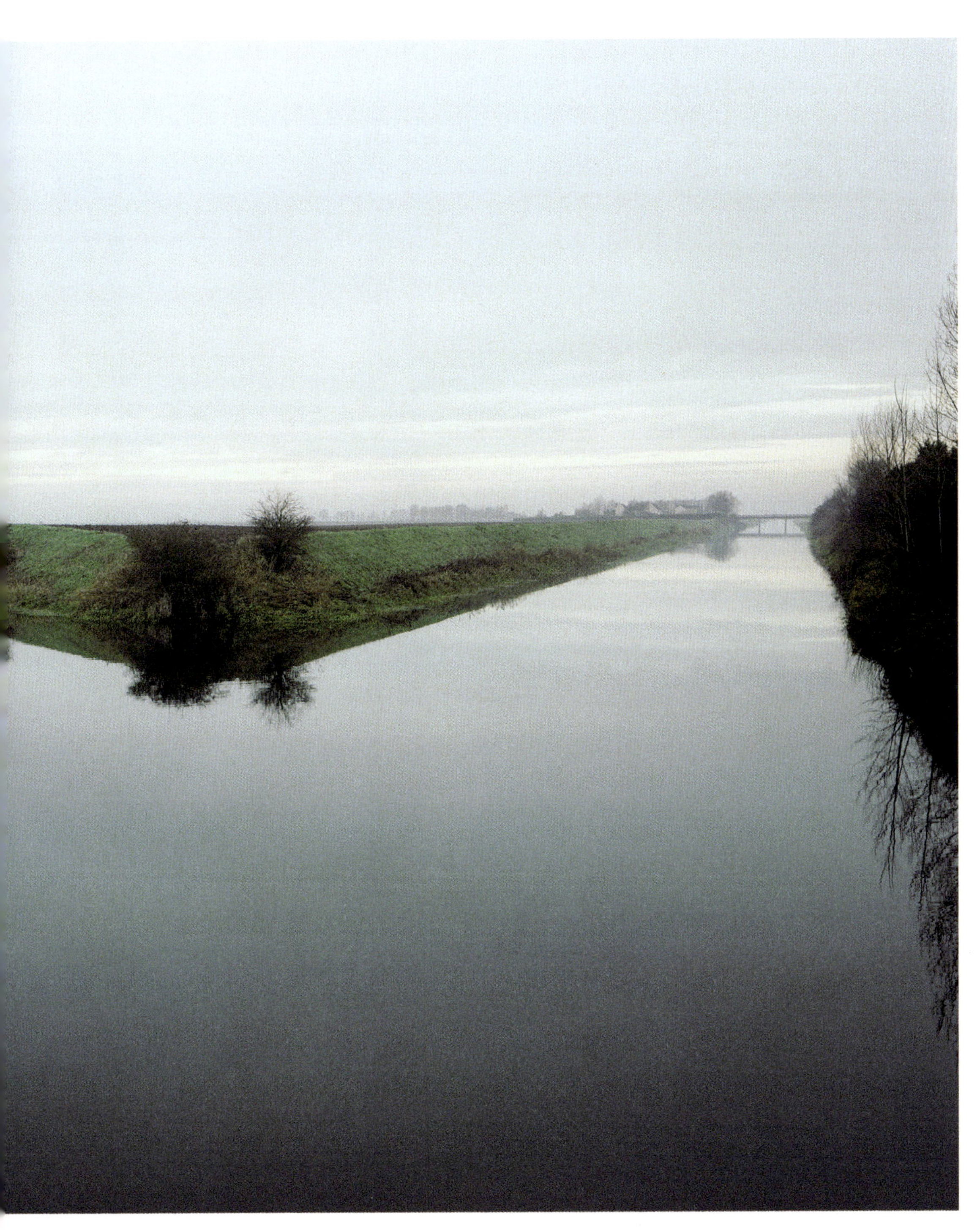

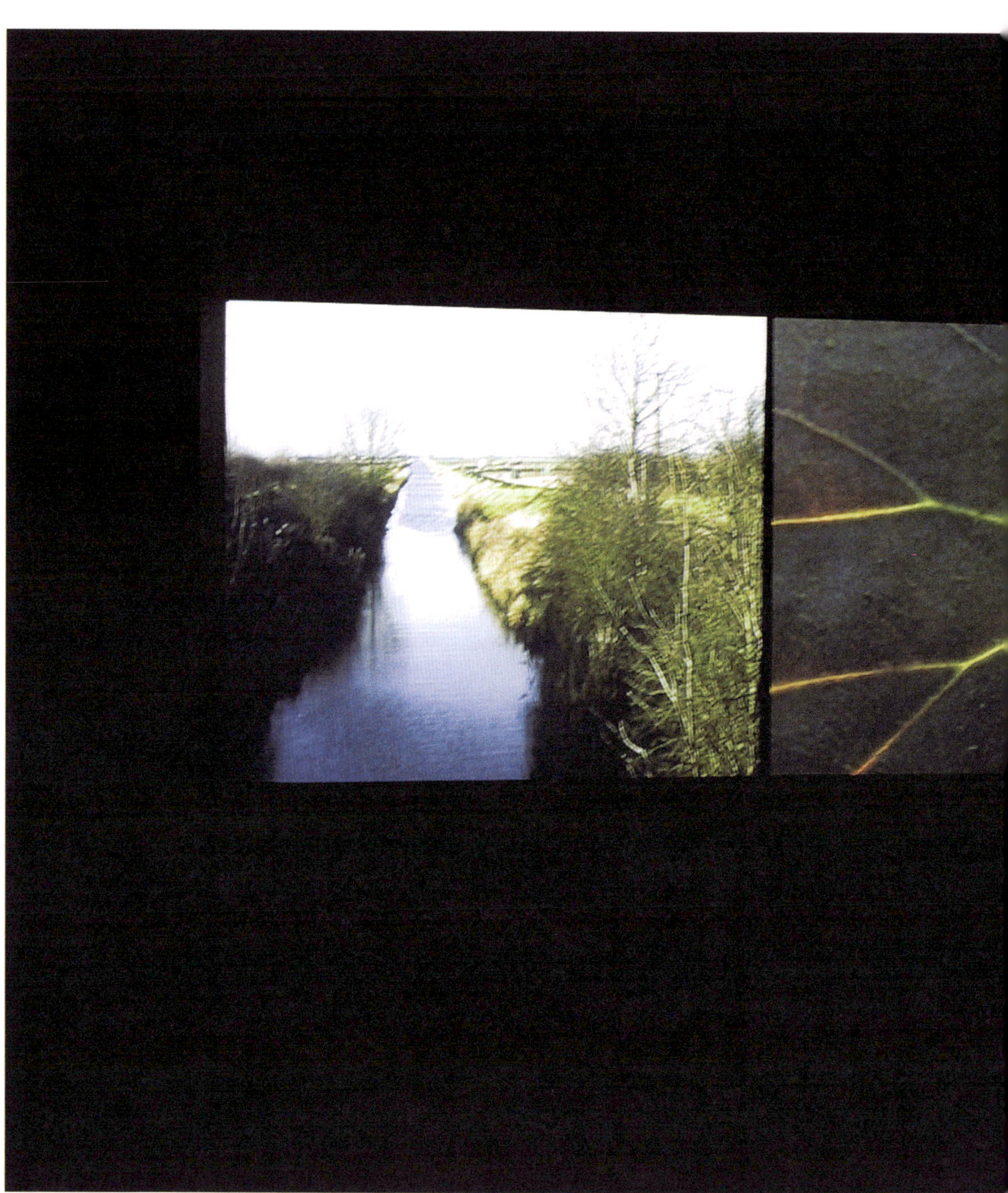

Dalziel + Scullion *Earthdom*

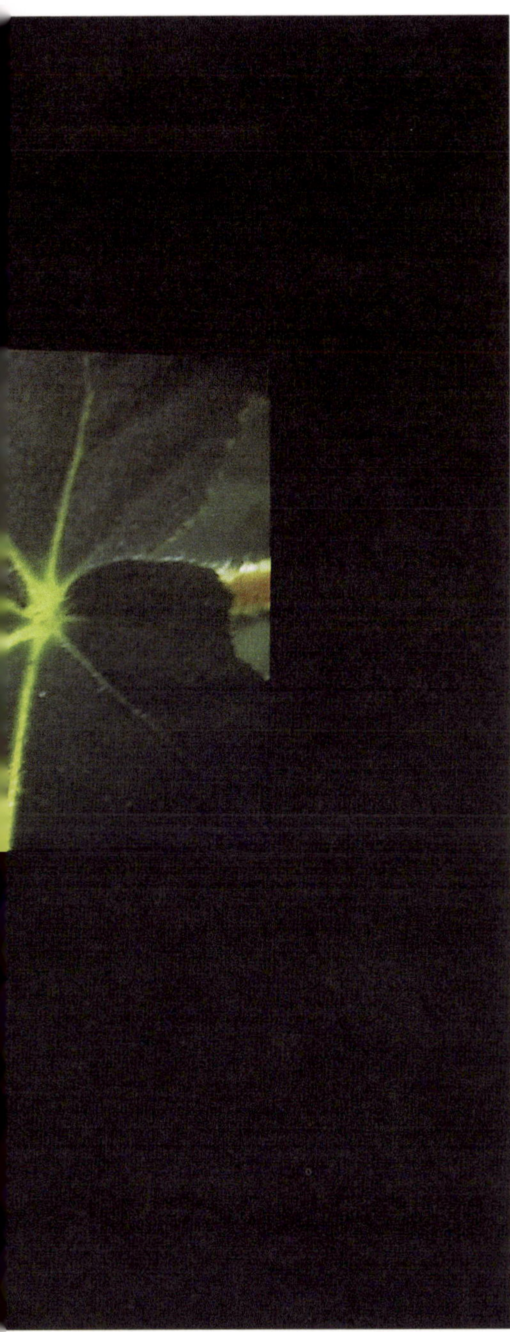

economic ties that now exist between Britain and the United States), their coming-into-existence inaugurated a boom of speculation, and high-wire market expansion, that also seems strangely familiar to 21st century eyes.

In their up-to-the-minute hi-tech hothouses, busily incubating a brave new future, the movers and shakers of Silicon Fen may not dwell too long on the history of the region, and care even less; the so-called 'leading edge' is rarely moved forward by being mired in lingering attachments to the past. Nonetheless, there is much in this haunting and strangely reverberant part of the country (whose isolation is actually somewhat deceptive) to prompt wider reflection: on the earlier groundbreaking precedent of the building of the canals, and on the ambivalent, often fraught co-existence of nature and human artifice; on the virtues, and triumphs, of human ingenuity, and on the future scope, and the likely limits, of our obsession with progress.

History is all too quickly forgotten, perhaps, but nature is not so easily dispensed with. It is interesting to note that the draining of the Fens did not immediately subjugate the natural forces that had shaped the landscape for centuries, but merely shifted the ceaseless interplay between man and the elements to a different level. As computer networks and smart technologies promote an ever more abstracted, virtual existence, it may be that a similar equilibrium needs to be discovered within today's technologically adapted and sophisticated environment. In this, it is fascinating to observe how a number of recent technological innovations appear to emulate, in one form or other, natural phenomena or processes; or, at very least, take their names or organising principles from natural metaphors or associations. Along this part of the Silicon frontier that has sprung up on the borders of Fenland (where the flow of data mirrors the flow of water, and where wireless clouds turn to the skies for inspiration) technology finds myriad echoes in the adjoining landscape. The pages that follow (and the artists' projects presented in them) offer a guide to where best to look.

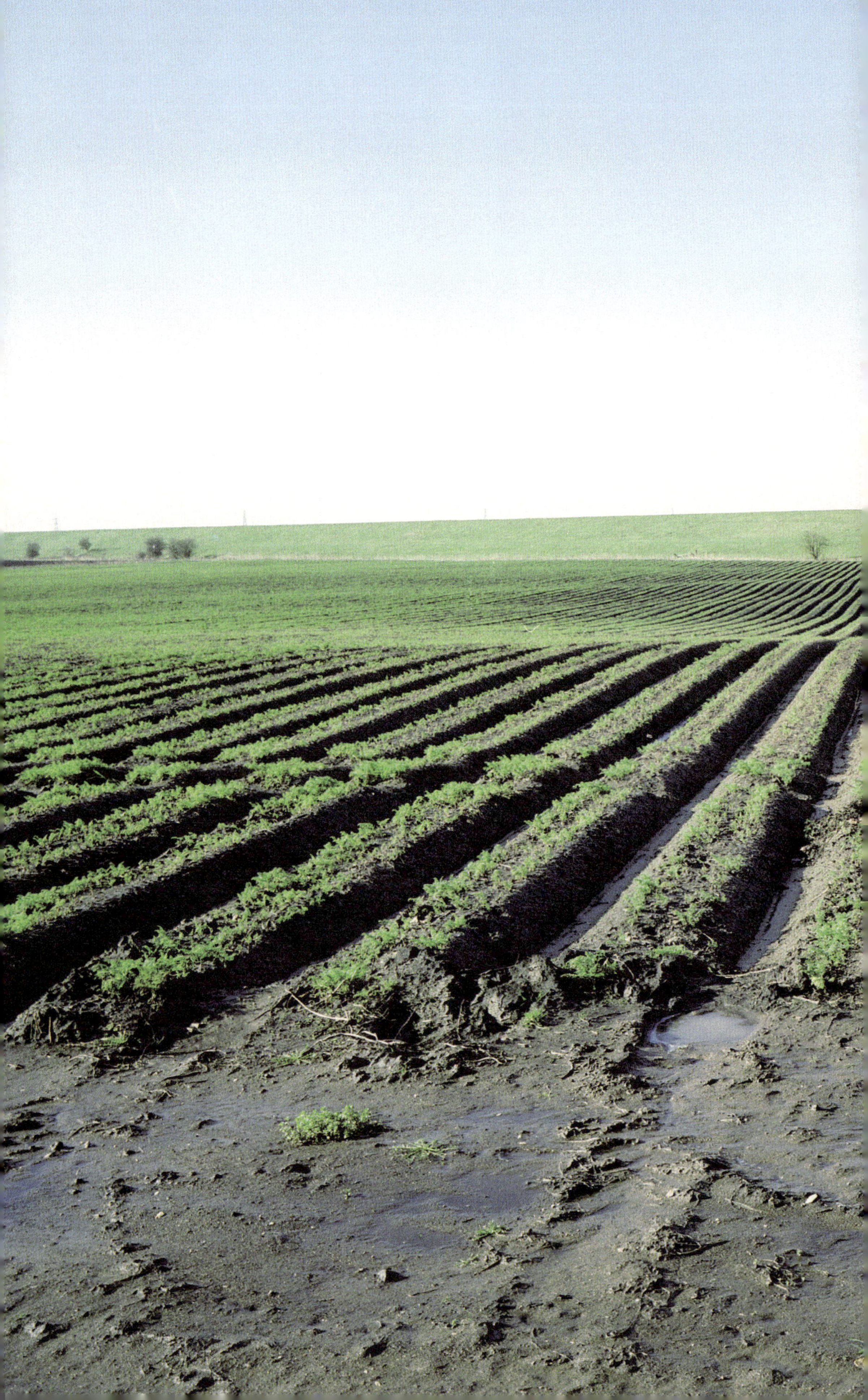

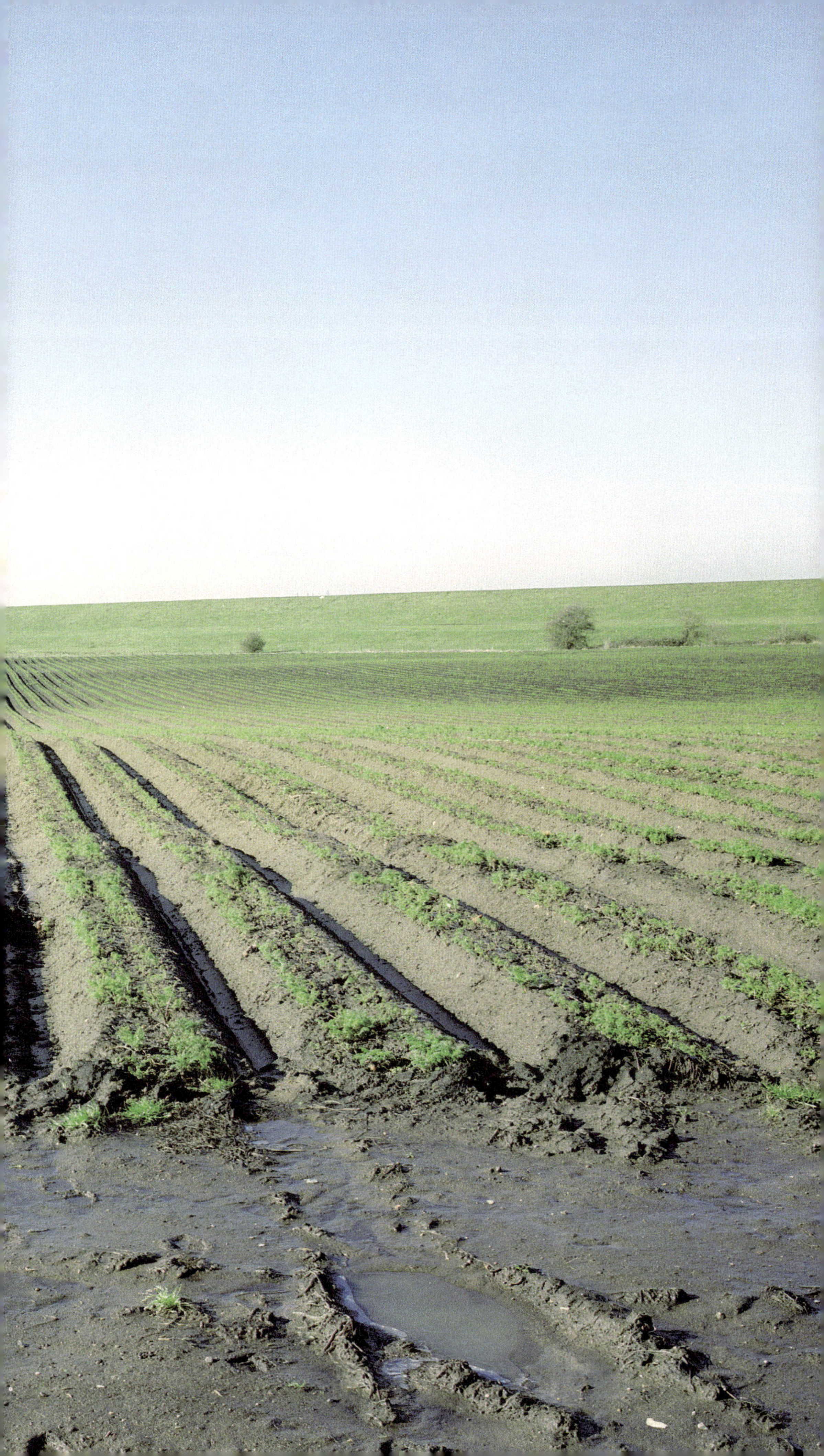

The Landscape Disturbance Sean Cubitt

The Speckleby rector is said to be mad

It stretches away. The sky is immense. A few miles north,
Cambridgeshire gives way invisibly to Lincolnshire, as if to prove that
boundaries have nothing to do with landscape. Underfoot some
of the richest agricultural land in Europe, overhead a generously
fertile, vast, ever-changing weather-scape. Between them, the
biting wind off the North Sea, and the agricultural labourers whose
income for decades marked the minimum wage in England. Where
Tess of the D'Urbervilles, at her nadir, is discovered pulling turnips
from half-frozen clay. A landscape of enduring solidity, of earth and
clay, slowly giving way to limestone at the soft rise of the Lincoln
Wold, of water in the air, underfoot, in the drainage ditches, in
ponds and rivers, and of air, wind and cloud in a vast half-globe
untouched overhead.

The sky remains immense. Across the Fens, they say, you were
never out of earshot of church bells, and spires and towers dot the
horizon. Growing up in the Fens was a time of newts and stickle-
backs, duckweed and frogspawn, chasing bats with torch beams
and prying into swallows' nests. Suky Best's delicate animations
recall that childhood, vignettes of landscapes where jewel-like
animations of species driven from the fens are restored to their
world. Swallowtails once again flutter over a mouldering tree stump,
echoed by the distant stump of Ely Cathedral; fritillaries battle the
East wind over the rusting wreckage of a tractor. The soundscapes,
partly location recordings, partly archival recordings of nightingale
song or the buzzing of rare bees, here and there the growl of traffic,
are pristine in their artifice. These are acts of kindness as much
as they are ecological arguments or moments of nostalgia that
nonetheless touch on the always tragic landscape of the fen. Kindness
for species that persist despite the grubbing out of hedges in pursuit
of agribusiness. Kindness in the root sense of 'kin', tendering a hand,
a gesture, to our mortal kind among the birds and insects.

And by implication a gesture of kinship with the earth and sky, brick and
wood, the mortal clay of which we're all composed. The colours of Best's video
palette, for example in the vignette of the Privet Hawks Moth larva making
its slow way along a fence rail, are a lesson in the paucity of our vocabularies
for colour, recalling Brakhage's query, back in 1963: 'How many colours are
there in a field of grass to the crawling baby unaware of 'Green'?'. You glimpse
a monochrome cream grey sky, the steel back of a sign, and infer rather than
see the greyed-out orange of plastic construction netting, and behind it a tiny

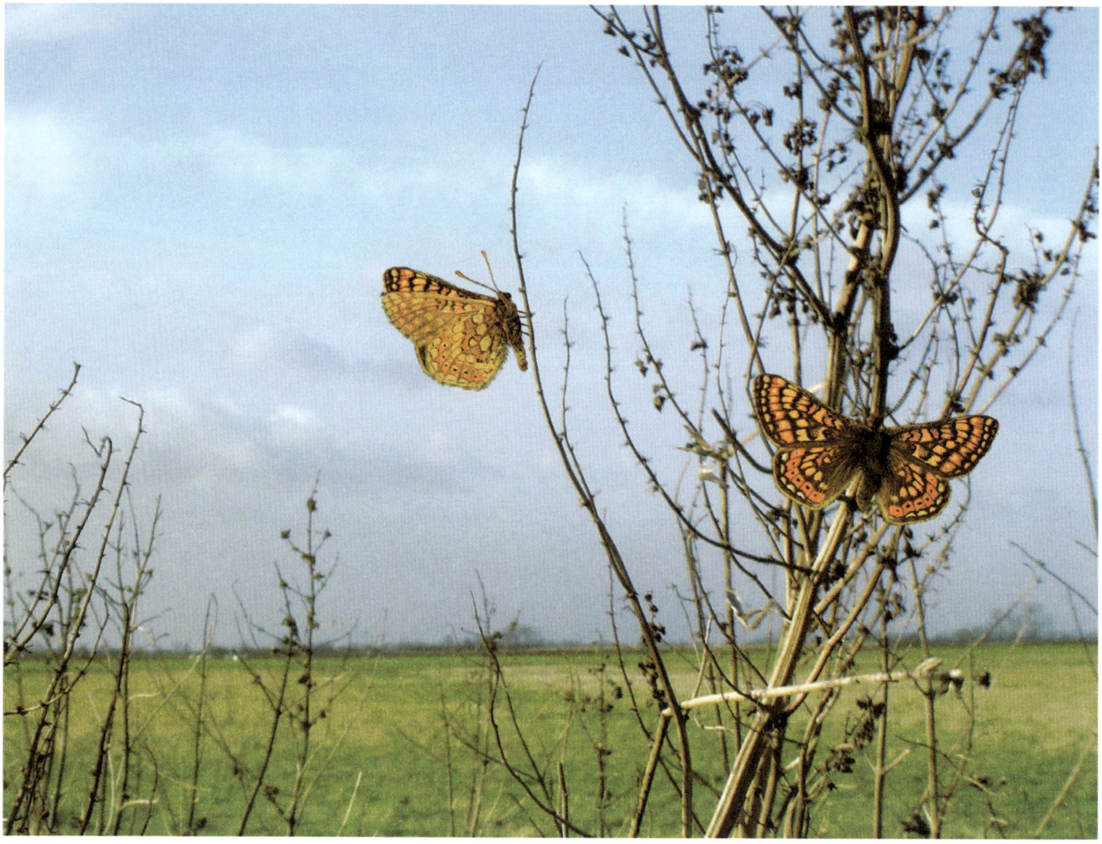

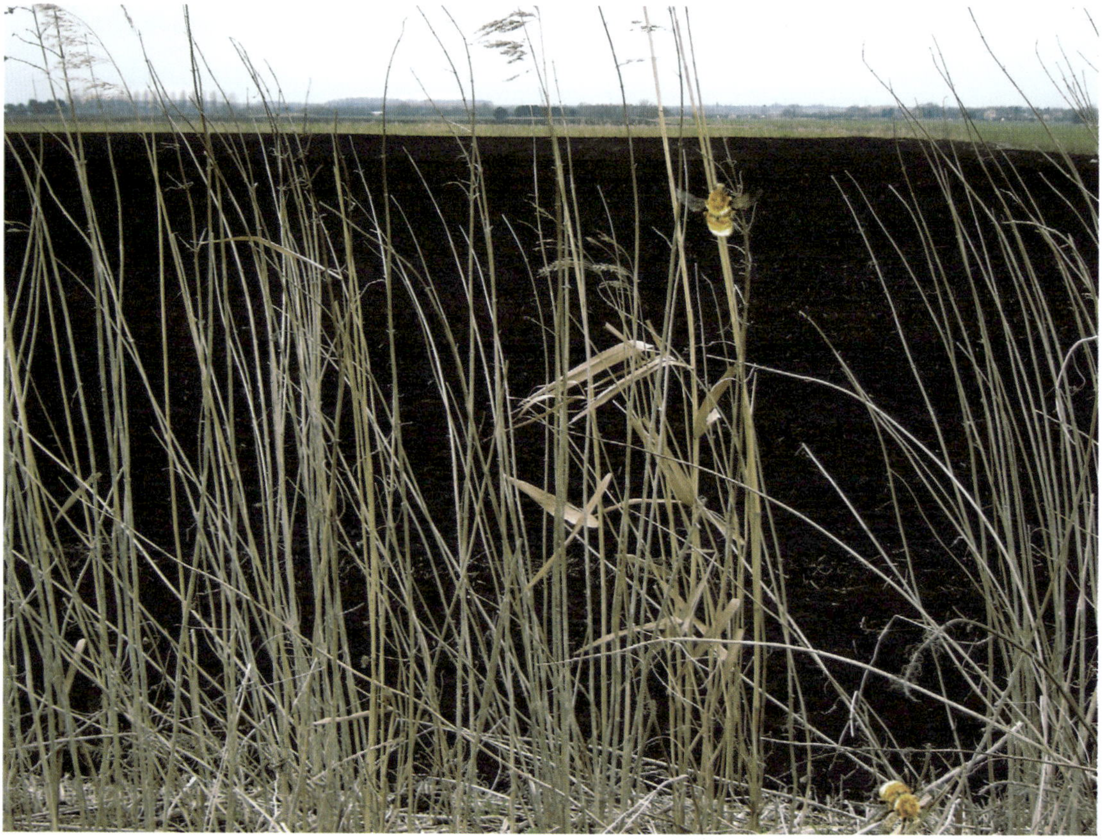

Suky Best *The Return of the Native*

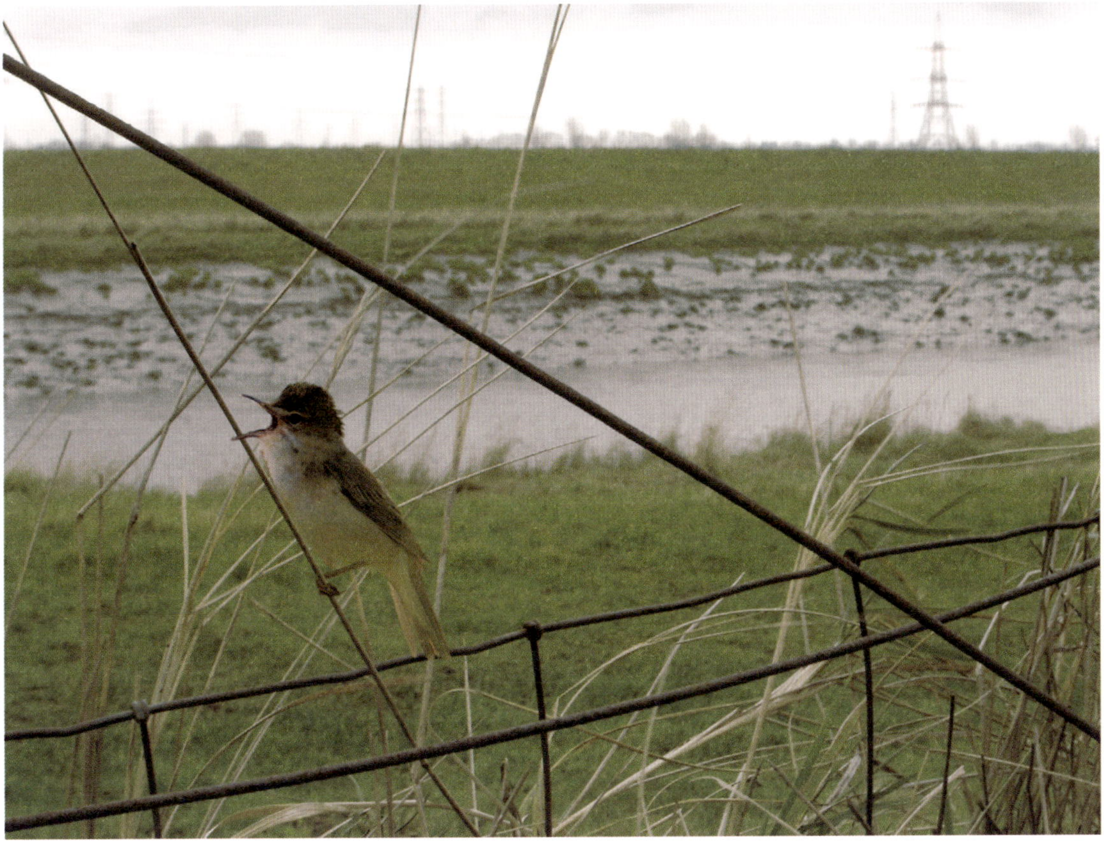

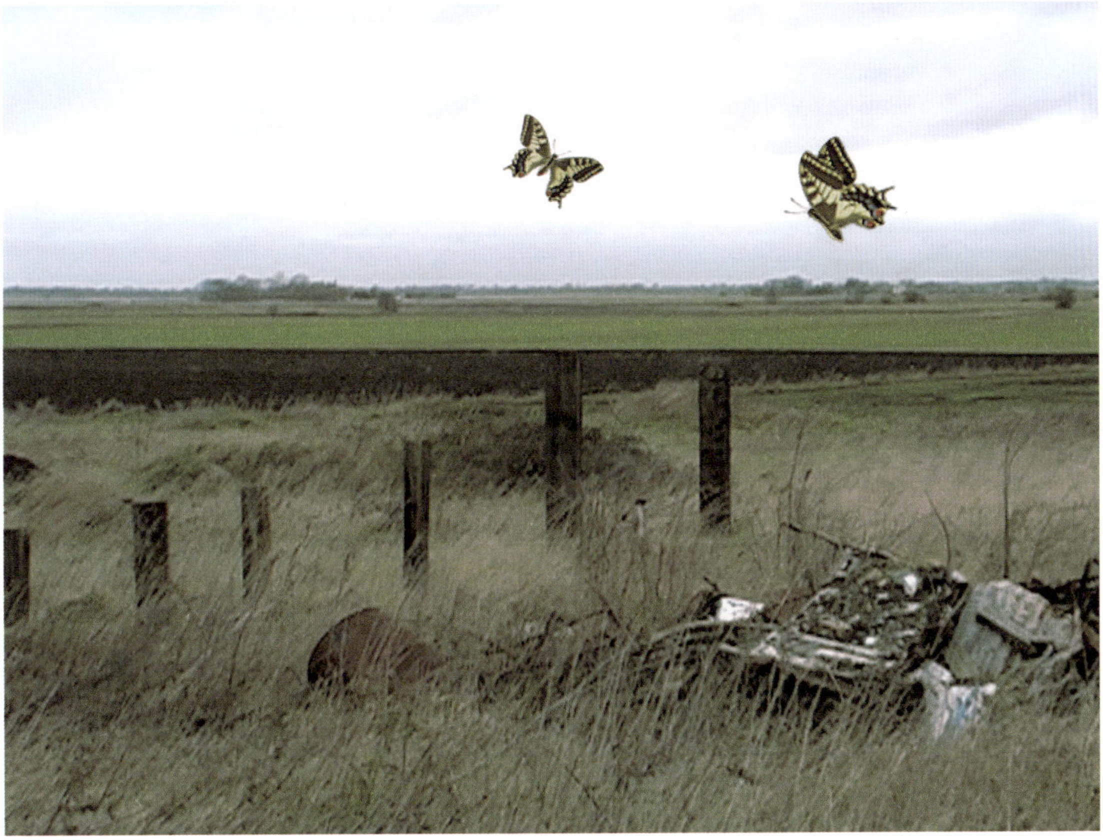

wilderness of grey-greens, silver-greens, leek-green and lime-tree-green, yellow-green and brown-green, pine-green and a green so highlit by the sky it seems white (but is, mechanically at least, the equivalent of Pantone Coated 578, a pastel, slightly earthy, slightly silver green you might find, perhaps, on certain moulds seen under a fluorescent tube). You want to say, the translucent, startling citrus green of the larva is an acid tone echoing the broad-leaved plant below it, save that that plant is veined with darker greens, and on its upper surfaces is greyer, dustier, and besides it trembles in the wind with a movement quite unlike the patient ripple of the larva walk. And then, passing in front of a denser agglomeration of reeds, the bug seems to change colour, though the colour itself remains the same, only shifting tone in relation to the immediate surround. Nature loves our abandoned nooks, and in tiny Edens and within the boundaries of green and grey, evolves infinitissimal infinities.

So too the patient unfurling of the webcam landscapes of Susan Collins' *Fenlandia*, gathered at the rate of a pixel a minute. The Hubble Space telescope features an optical device known as the photon counter. It gathers old light, grains of energy from the oldest, furthest, faintest stars, smeared from their millennium-long journey, holds them to itself, records their passage, probably absorbing the last of their ancient energy to do so. Collins' visual essay recalls that picking of quanta one by one, recording the state of light at that sole moment. One thinks of Monet taking six or seven canvases out to his favourite spots to record the light for ten minutes, then the next ten, and then return the next day to capture the same changing light, just after dawn, ten minutes after, twenty... That patience now can be gathered into the webcam, the patience of all the inventions and craft skills that it assembles from the sleeping anonymous ancestors whose work it now embodies: the patience of machinery, the patience of the dead, for ever at the service of the living. Here now they count, in real time, the pinpricks of illumination tilting at the selenium receptors in the camera's eye, carrying them miles and miles, or perhaps just the other side of a wall, from the big world to the small screen. Painting with light, of course, but painting which is endlessly attentive to the shifting tones, and to the strange alchemy of time and colour, how these russet earths shift in the course of an hour or sixty pixels, replacing one at a time the tones of those same places twenty-odd hours ago. And transforming them, once in the lens, once more in the screen, and one more time in the viewer's eye, but much more so in their relations to the field of colour that is the whole of the landscape image, and to the time that now inhabits it as this patiently, kindly evolving granular transciption. Nature submits more kindly to surveillance than we do. It has never been private.

And yet the natural world and natural processes have their secrets too. You infer, from the opening shot of the rapids, that *Earthdom* by Dalziel + Scullion is

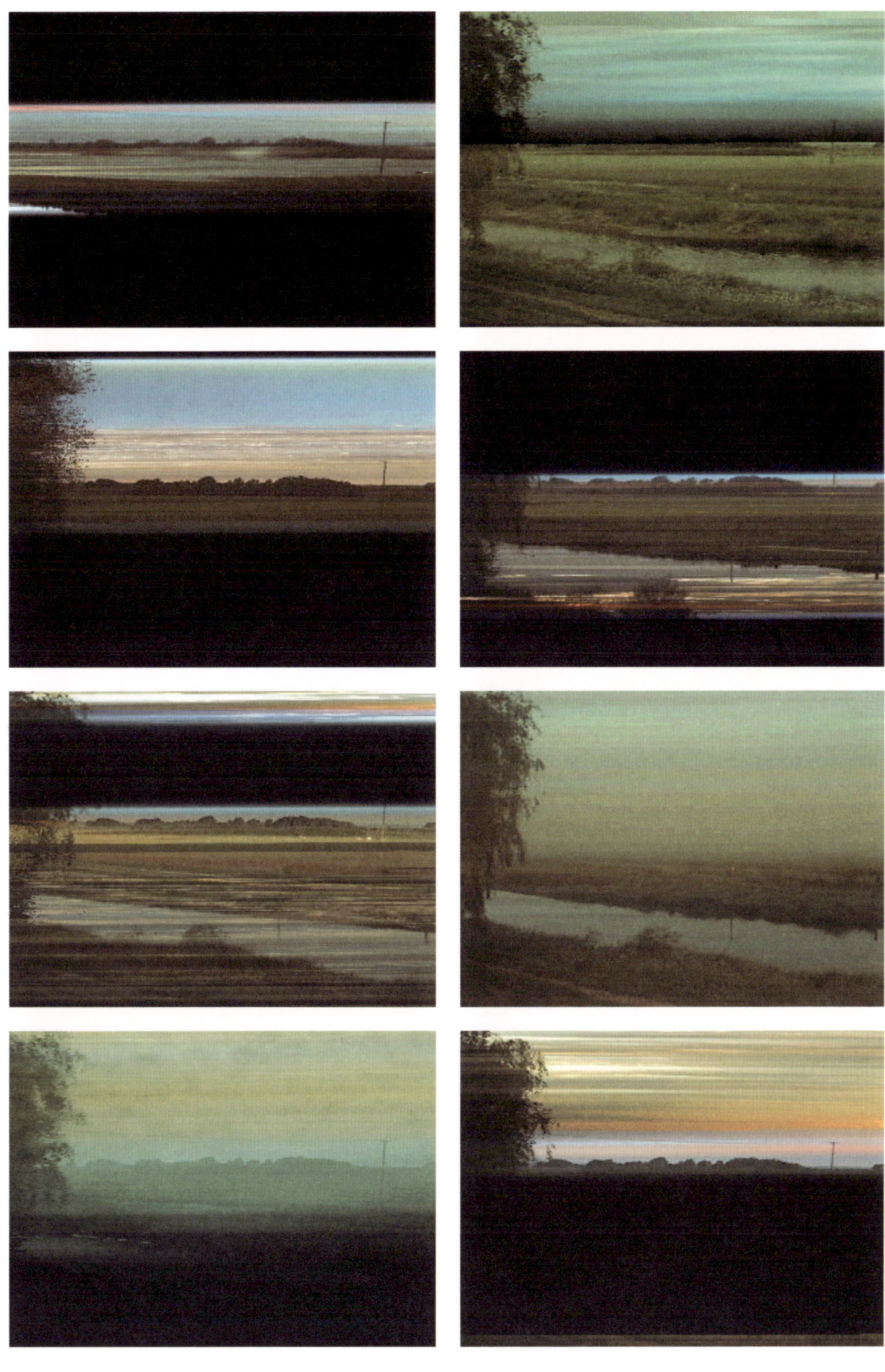

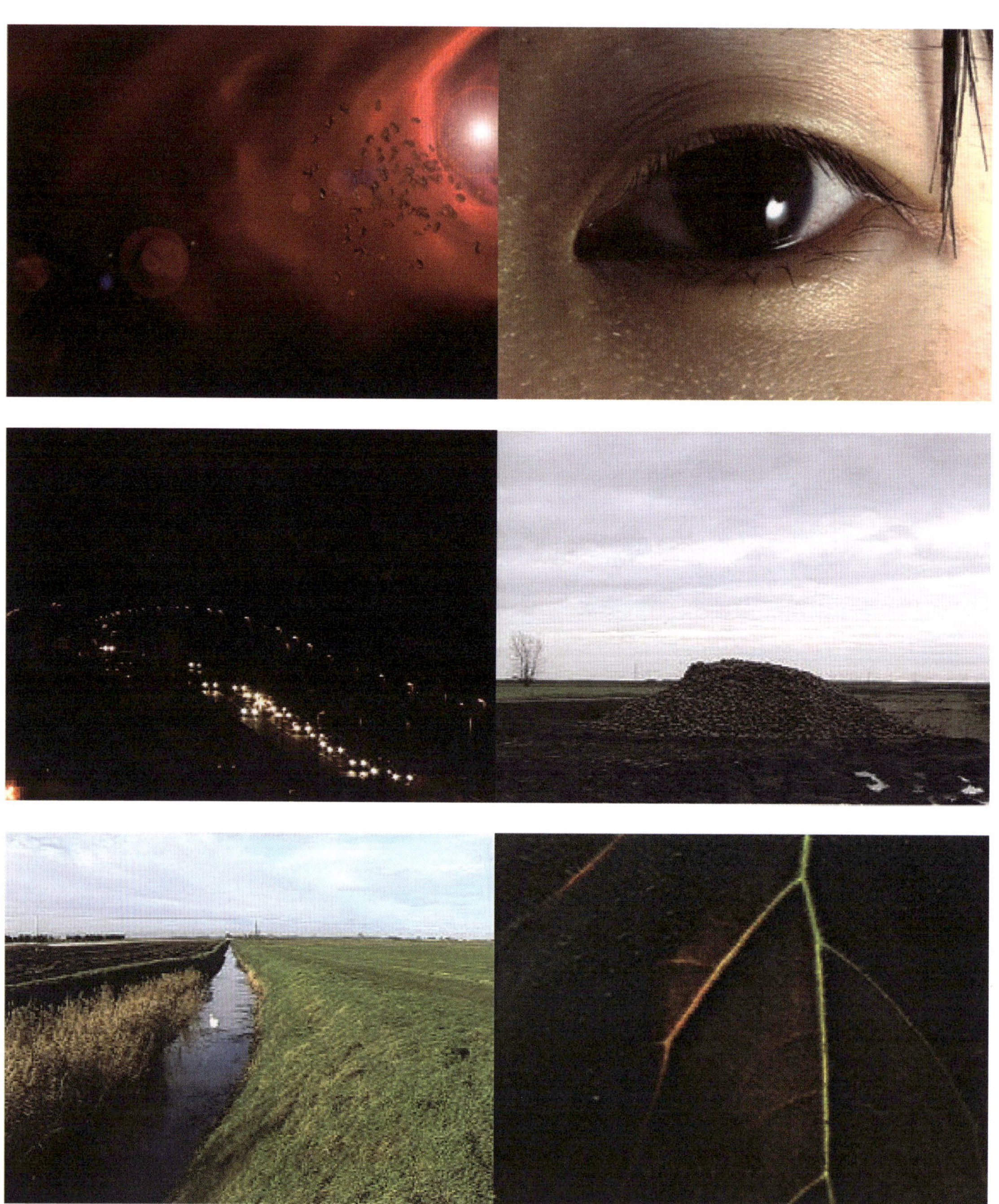

Dalziel + Scullion *Earthdom*

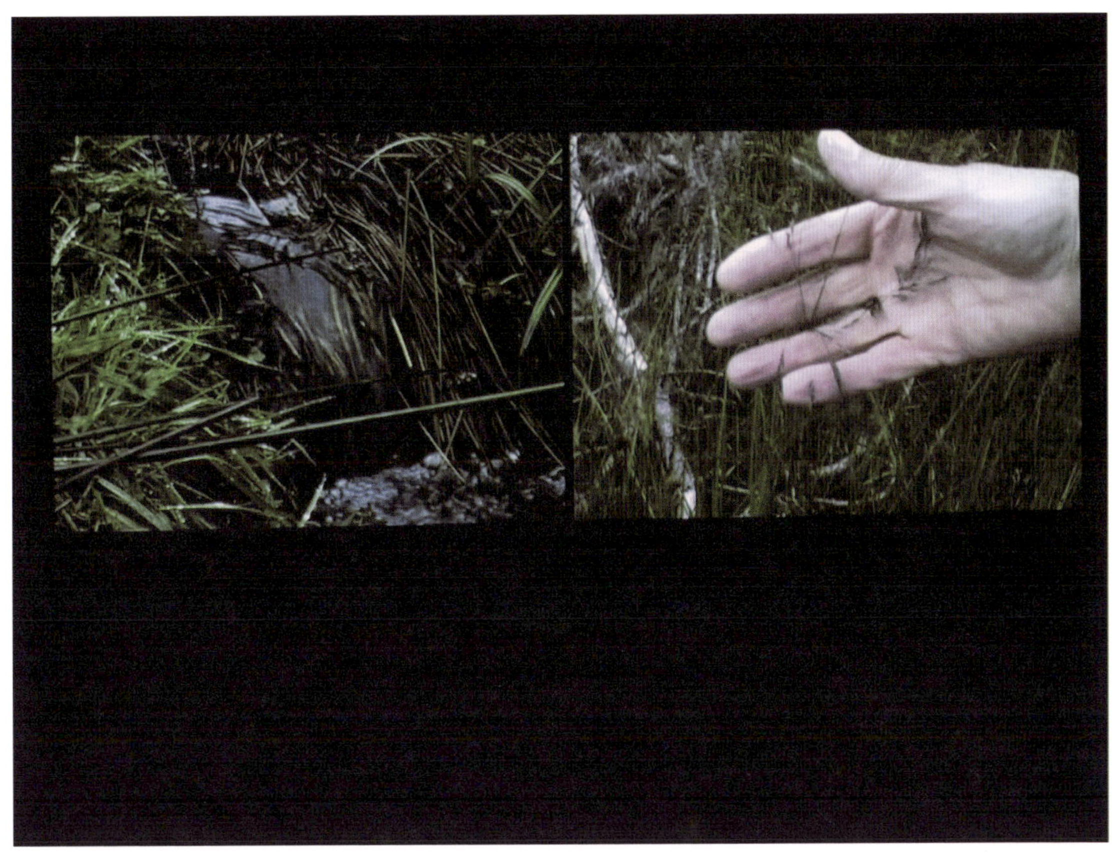

about a difference, between two water-made landscapes, the mountains that
force the river through the rocks and deck themselves with disappearing clouds,
and the all-alluvial fens. And then a third watery landscape, eyes, one bounded
with an epicanthic fold, one a horse's, two in the face of a young woman who
has been pirouetting on the spot in a school hall a moment before and who
now stands gently blinking in the camera's stare. The rush of mountain water
makes way, over a transition, to shots of still, wind-ruffled fenland dikes, on
one a swan floats, above her the skyline and perhaps the blue band of the
slow rise of the Lincoln Wold. And these give way to a brief 3D animation that
resembles that kind of *Scientific American* graphic that shows the haemoglobin
flowing through your veins, a Photoshop lens flare mirroring the reflection in
the eye on the paired screen, as the platelets ripple as if seen through a rippling
and refracting medium, a digital water, a dangerous contradiction of electricity
and moisture that nonetheless forms the aqueous medium of the eye, the wet
interior of the brain that is itself in the process of becoming a landscape for
scientific imaging. If that suggests a certain cold objectivity, recall the emergence
of ecology as a new kind of science, a systems-based vision in which information
flows as surely as water or current, the world as feedback, boundary state,
signal. If Suky Best makes the world miraculous in detail, Dalziel + Scullion
make it miraculous in its connectivity.

A thought that perhaps also shapes Annabel Howland's photographs,
abstractions in the sense that science abstracts from the flux of the world its
numerical shapes. She abstracts its geometries, the shapes left when you have
removed culture, agriculture (in the same way that Ezra Pound remarked once

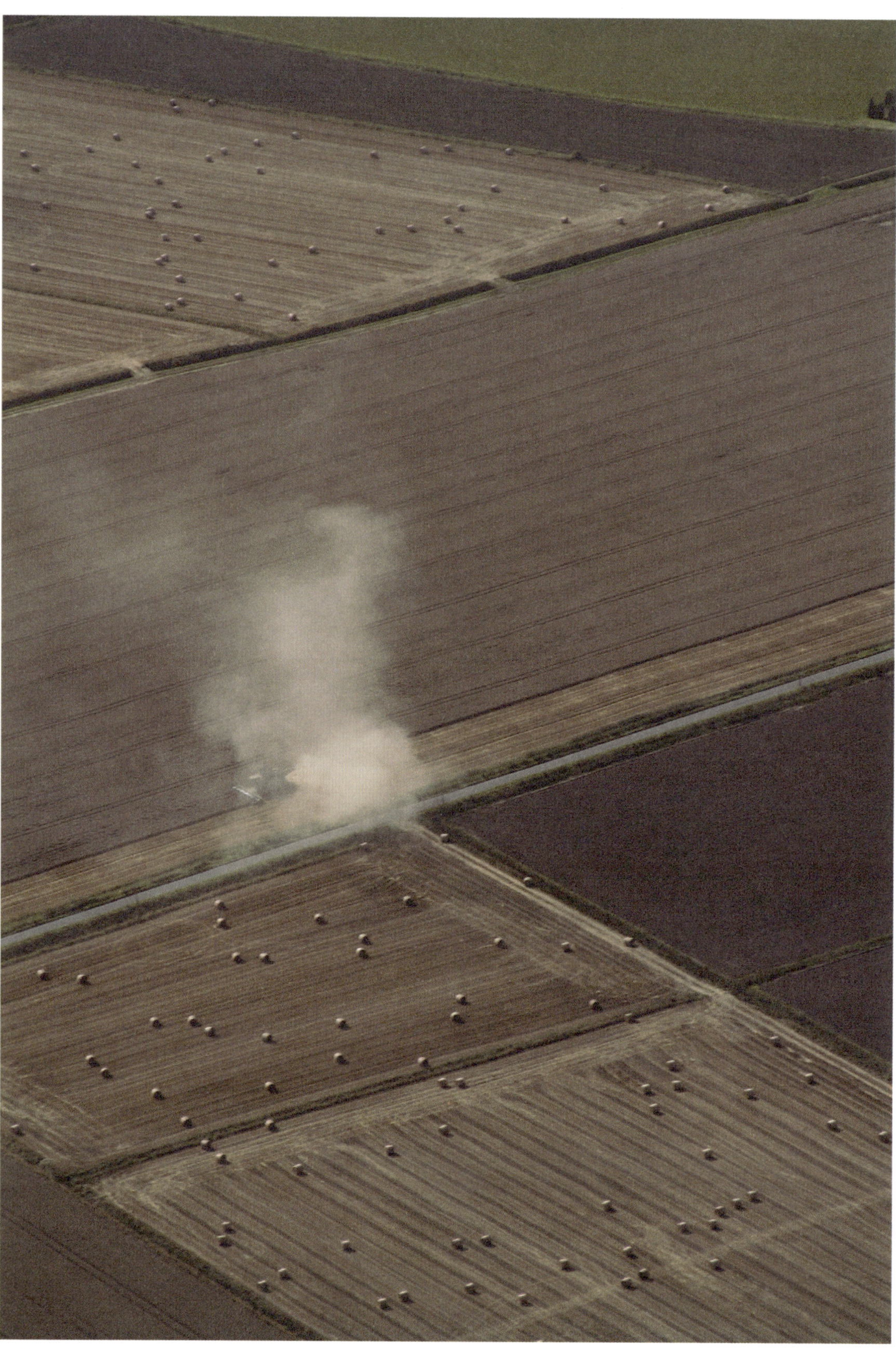

Annabel Howland *Drains, Cables, and Cuts*
Opposite top – Annabel Howland still from animation *Cut Drains, Charts, Creeks and Cuts*

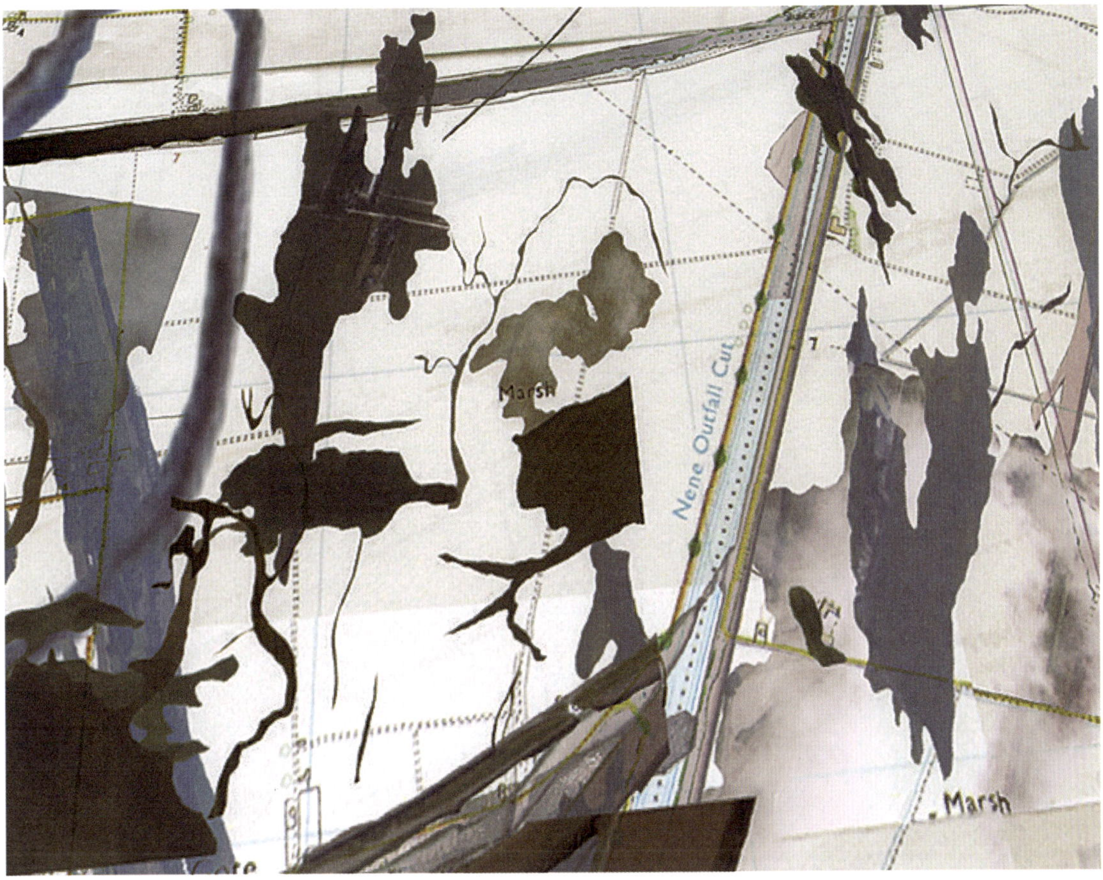

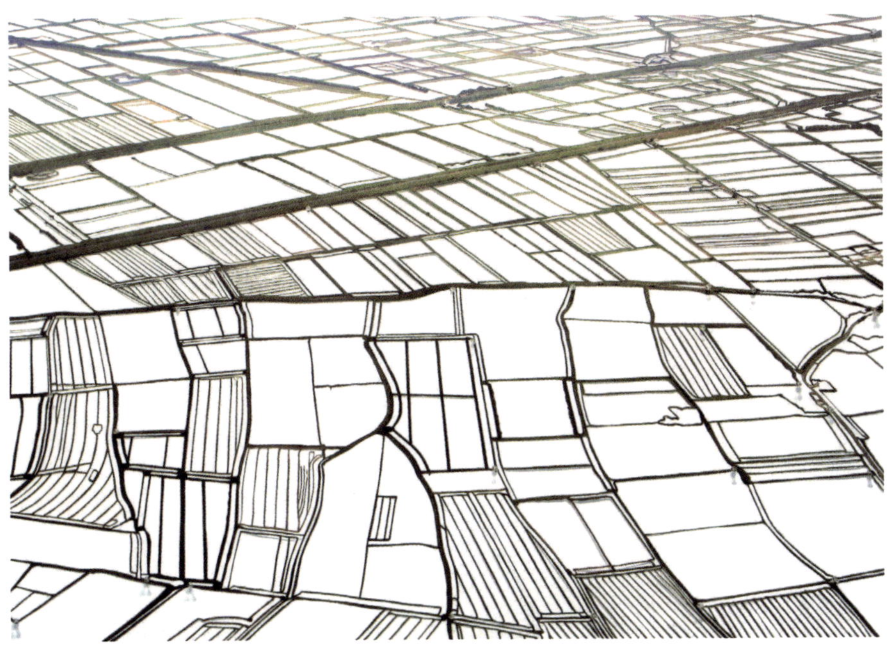

Marsh
Nene Outfall Cut
Marsh

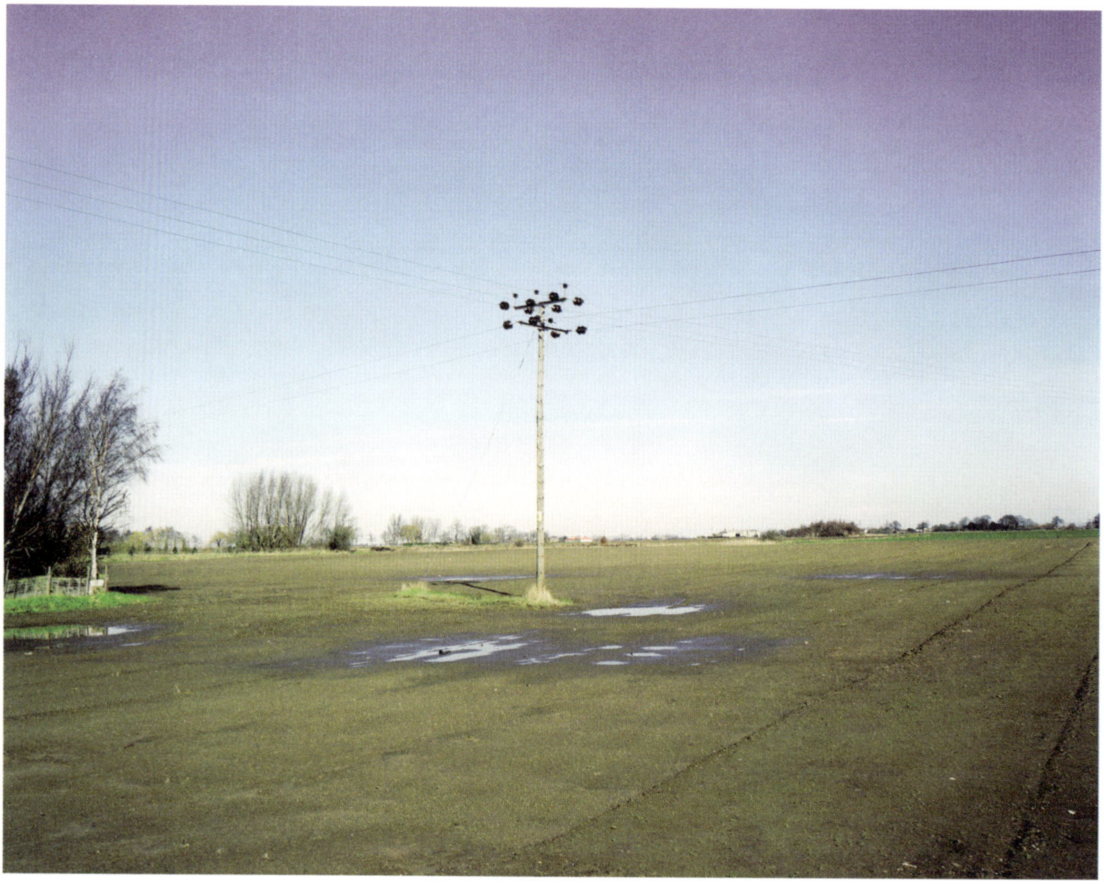

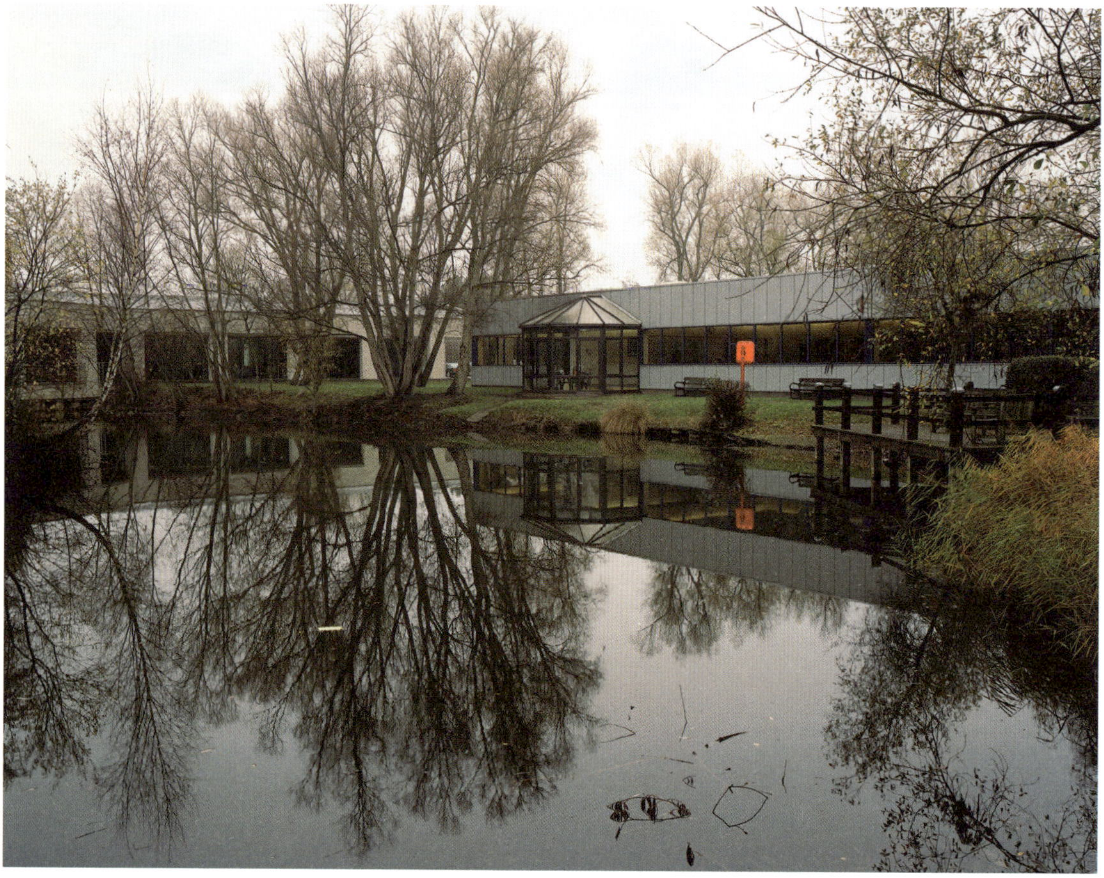

Stephen Hughes *Untitled*

that culture was what was left after you had forgotten which book), and left only its traces on the landscape as seen from the air. You look at the big cibachrome of a blizzard obscuring a corner of the fens, the kind of '*effet de gelée*' that Pissarro loved, alongside these cartographic skeletons, the bones beneath the skin, the lines of the dykes, and the obscure traces of buried diggings and old waterways, and you see other obscurities and other miracles for bringing them to the light. Seen from above, our world is both a rich mosaic of lines and patches, and at the same time touchingly human. The animation *Cut Drains, Charts, Creeks and Cuts* flies over a paper landscape, in which from time to time the lines resolve into drawings, into photographs of landscapes that abut their mapped depiction. Areas of the map are obscured by photographs of clouds. You instinctively trust the artist that these clouds were observed at these grid references, that the obscuration is a record of a real obscurity, and a real revelation of cloud over the fens. Part of the imagery derives from a flight in a retired World War Two aircraft, from the era of aerial photography. Now the ante has been upped, and planes are restricted to the military to be re-placed in the sciences by earth-observation satellites. The military remains: Howland uses the Ordnance Survey maps, whose name derives from their original intention, to provide the artillery with reliable terrain maps. But here there is not only no war but no terrain: a paucity of gradient lines for this flatness. Instead, a landscape of colour, inchoate as it seems seen side on from the ground, but revealing its archeological geometry to the airborne. Although in the animation the flight is only virtual, it reveals an archipelago of trails and boundaries, zones where layers of surface features, photographs, clouds and map symbols stain each other like water stains paper, a blue and blue-grey tabletop world whose pink patches and terminal edge arrive like the shock of the first bird before dawn.

In the photography of Stephen Hughes, the camera's line of sight is horizontal, in the sense that it frames horizons. In the lurid purples of the image above left, the electric-water catastrophe is held apart by a telegraph pole, its foot in a clump of grass in a field where ponds of surface water catch the magic hour light like sheet metal, in irregular patches. The array of ceramic junctions look like some science fiction prop under a sky from another planet. The mirror pond in front of an anonymous low-rise building in another photo catches the bare willows, the fenced and therefore purposeless jetty, the starkly ornamental conservatory, the tiny dab of red from a council-regulation lifebelt stand, but the waters are cracked with loops of black that might be twigs and branches, or might be wire and traps. Whether looking at the geometric curve of a glass-frontage bordered by plantings of introduced trees and rock-like shrubs, or the wet, black ploughed field disappearing into mist, your eye wanders into the scene as through an open window, sensing the

tactility of the place, its very smell of cold, wet loam, only to find, there at
the back of the image, a blank wall, a blockage, a seduction concluded
with a sudden chill. In every image there is evidence of people, and like the
Impressionists, there's a fascination with the ways light industry has marched
step by step into the marginal spaces between suburb and countryside. This
rich dark soil gives the lie to the appellation 'greenfield site'. At first you think
you've found the exception, a holt of winter trees, some fallen, all dredged in
ivy, a messy place, at least one tree in the slow process of falling through the
resisting branches of its neighbour, and in the foreground one so fallen. But
what is this stray smudge of yellow on the tall, green upright? Is this a tree
or some kind of pole, with some kind of message, some further trace of the
ubiquitous human hand that marks every inch of the fen? Like tyre tracks in
the mud, the photographs themselves mark these as human spaces, places
where an action has taken place, a human story, however banal, or human
work has gone on or goes on. Too cold and damp for any but the most Middle
European of cinematic narratives, you can in every instance imagine a television
journalist entering the frame from one side or another, approaching the camera,
looking straight into the lens, and addressing you on some invisible quality of
the scene: 'You would scarcely guess to look at it, but this is the place where…
England's only gold mine lies, the last English beaver was killed, the future of
computing is being constructed'. A secret world, or one that guards its secrets.

The great tradition of landscape is, the landscape historians tell us, very
short. Much more than the West, the Chinese adored the retreat into the
mountains. Europe hated them, and fields were for peasants. The *Très Riches
Heures du Duc de Berry* that the Limbourg Brothers painted for him in the
fifteenth century never seems to leave the castle grounds, and when most
remote peppers the landscape with ducal waymarkers and patron saints.
And as Warncke has it, the landscape remains from then on brutally political,
whether at war or peace. What's more, it returns forever, as it had been in the
Middle Ages and for Bunyan and Dante, as allegory. The Barbizon School's
praying peasants in the field portray the natural piety and destined place of
the poor as surely as the Limbourgs' February peasants, hiking their skirts to
warm their ankles directly under the spire of the hillside church.

What then is so remarkable is the persistence of such political themes
here in the 21st century: political with a small 'p'. For Best, and in some residual
way for all the artists in *Silicon Fen*, the fens are in some way the privileged
round on which the relation between agriculture, town-dwelling and wildlife
has framed the evolution of the region for a handful of hundred years. There
is a certain stillness in the moving image, a certain movement in the still,
that Best, Hughes, and perhaps most of all Collins share in their approaches
to this relation. In Howland's work, it is not the image that moves but

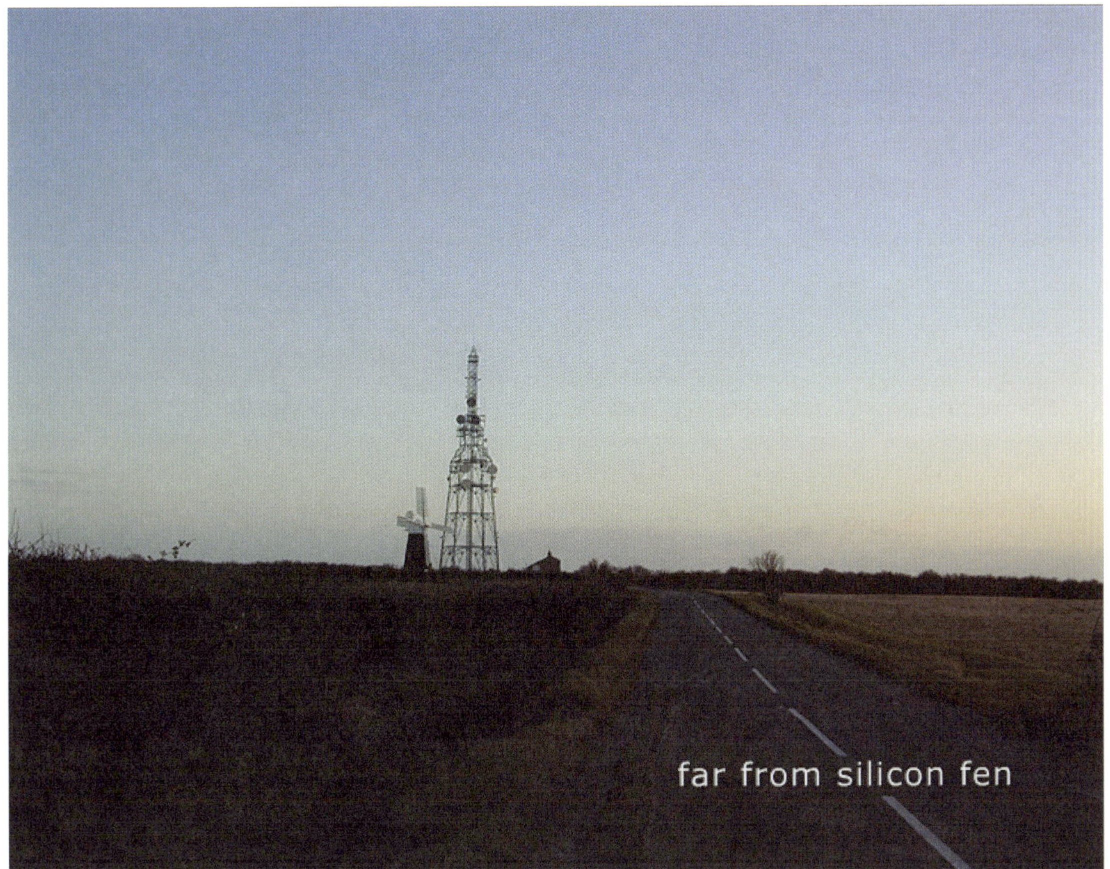

history, which recreates itself as a kind of geometry, of course, but also a
geology, one that requires a kind of looking that takes time as surely as
the landscapes they describe take place. In Dalziel + Scullion's *Earthdom* the
planet lives and breathes. Of all the works here, it is the one in which the *polis*,
the city, the social world seems most remote. It is instead a utopian space, a
dialogue between two screens, an ideal of a commonwealth where organic
and inorganic speak to one another in harmonious discords, the kinds that
bring about the rhythms of breath and blood.

Which is perhaps the cue for the final work in the show, TNWK's *far from
silicon fen*, a non-interactive website. It is a poem, says the writer: using the
random techniques pursued by the surrealists, now mechanised in Google,
replacing key terms with the phrase 'silicon fen' to make jokes, and to release
the tensions that arise, inevitably, when the beauty or degradation of nature
seems to get in the way of speaking about what nature harbours or shows.
'The inhabitants of Silicon Fen eke out a meagre living designing one another's
websites' they tell us, as a babble of voices threads through the strains of
'The Girl I Left Behind Me', that ancient song of the migrant labourer. Migration,
after all, was our species' first way of life, and it is becoming so again. No longer
living where we work or working where we live, no longer tied by feudal
bonds to a land that shrugs us off with every change of use, attracted instead
to the glistening future promised behind those sheet glass walls, or to the far
horizon where we will be refused by those we go to live amongst, nomads
again, for whom the landscape will always have the weight of memories that
were never ours.

This is the landscape of 'Silicon Fen', or rather its landscape art. Itself a sprawling transductor chip, as Howland shows so clearly, a network of linkages and sinks stretched from the nanotubule to stupendous acres of hummus and ditch, it is as if it throws itself at the digital lens in a fit of recognition. But it is, as always, a misrecognition too: there is an irreducible remainder to the interplays of the natural and the technological: it is the human, a film across the picture plane, a boundary. What disappears at the ever-present horizon is that old surety of who we are and where we live. These spaces and places variously hiding and revealing their subtleties and secrecies: these x-ray visions of their bones and qualities or, more truthfully, their absolute surfaces, their radiant temporality, this ephemeral world at the brink of disappearance, on the edge of becoming: this miraculous banality and banal miracle, is our terrain as surely as the clay and water, the electricity and sky that anchor us in the muck with our beer and tractors where we at once belong and do not belong, from which we are exiled but to which we forever look back, Adams yearning simultaneously for innocence, and to fall again.

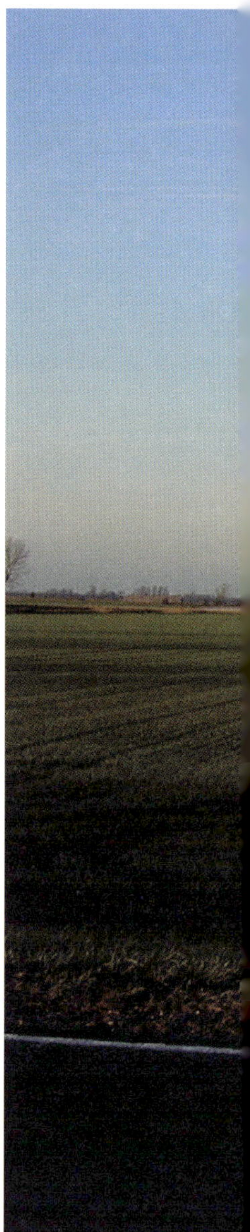

TNWK *far from silicon fen*

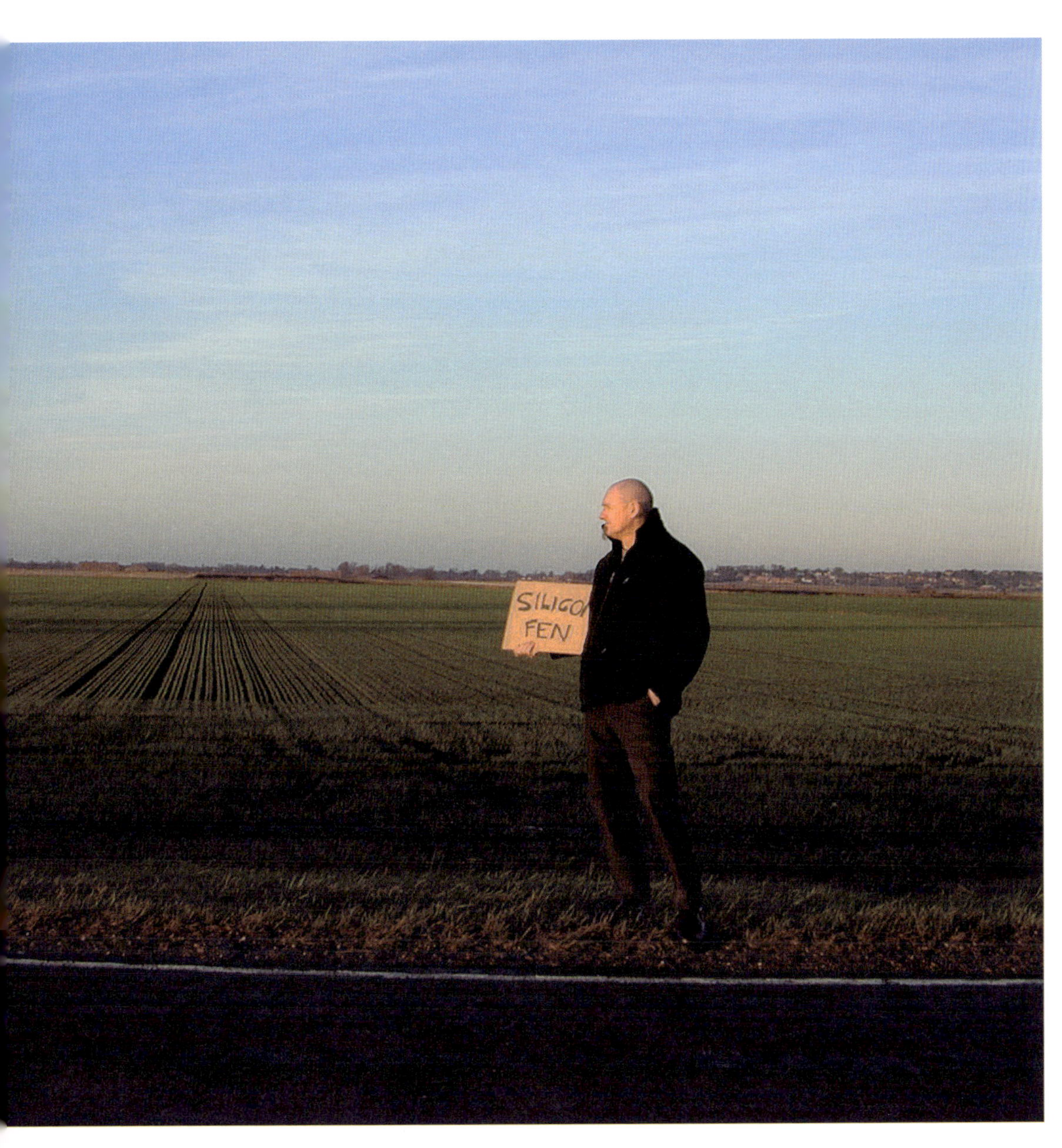

SILICON
FEN

Some people like the Fens, some people loathe them: few could honestly say that they *love* this most man-made of all landscapes, with its wide skies and level expanses of ploughland stretching to the far horizon. There are no elegant country houses or manicured parklands in the Fens: even after they had been converted from a wet wilderness to rich farmland, few eighteenth or nineteenth-century gentlemen would choose to live there. The extensive yet level panoramas offended contemporary ideas of landscape aesthetics and malaria-bearing mosquitoes continued to breed in the drainage dykes. Twentieth-century commentators have been no more enthusiastic. Graham Swift, for example, memorably describing the area as having a landscape which 'of all landscapes approximates most closely to nothing':

> *Flat, with an unrelieved and monotonous flatness... it stretched away to the horizon, its uniform colour, peat-black, varied only by the crops that grew upon it – grey-green potato leaves, blue-green beet, yellow-green wheat; its uniform levelness broken only by the furrowed and dead-straight lines of the ditches and drains.*

Nevertheless, the landscape has to many a certain idiosyncratic appeal; and to the historian the Fens are unquestionably bursting with interest, and much more varied than they first appear. Their story, moreover, curiously parallels that of the new industries of 'Silicon Fen': for its distinctive landscape was shaped, above all, by international contacts, and by progressive refinements in technology.

What we call 'The Fens' is in reality two quite distinct landscapes. There is an important distinction between the fields and settlements to be found in the area lying immediately inland from the Wash, on the silt soils, and the main area of fens, lying inland on the peat. The former was settled at an early date and by the Middle Ages contained substantial villages, large parish churches, and extensive areas of farmland. Villages had been established on the slightly higher ground, close to the sea, by the start of the twelfth century: expansion then occurred inland, onto the lower silt ground, the reclaimed land being protected from inundation by a series of substantial 'walls' or banks. The new fields took an unusual form, which still survives, although much simplified, in the modern landscape. They comprised bundles of long, parallel strips, each seldom more than twenty metres in width yet in some cases as much as two kilometres long. These remarkable landscapes resemble, very closely, those created by eleventh, twelfth and thirteenth-century reclamation on the peat lands of Holland, especially North Holland. How far this was the consequence of parallel development, how far the large landowners – especially monasteries – which directed much of the reclamation work actually brought in Dutch

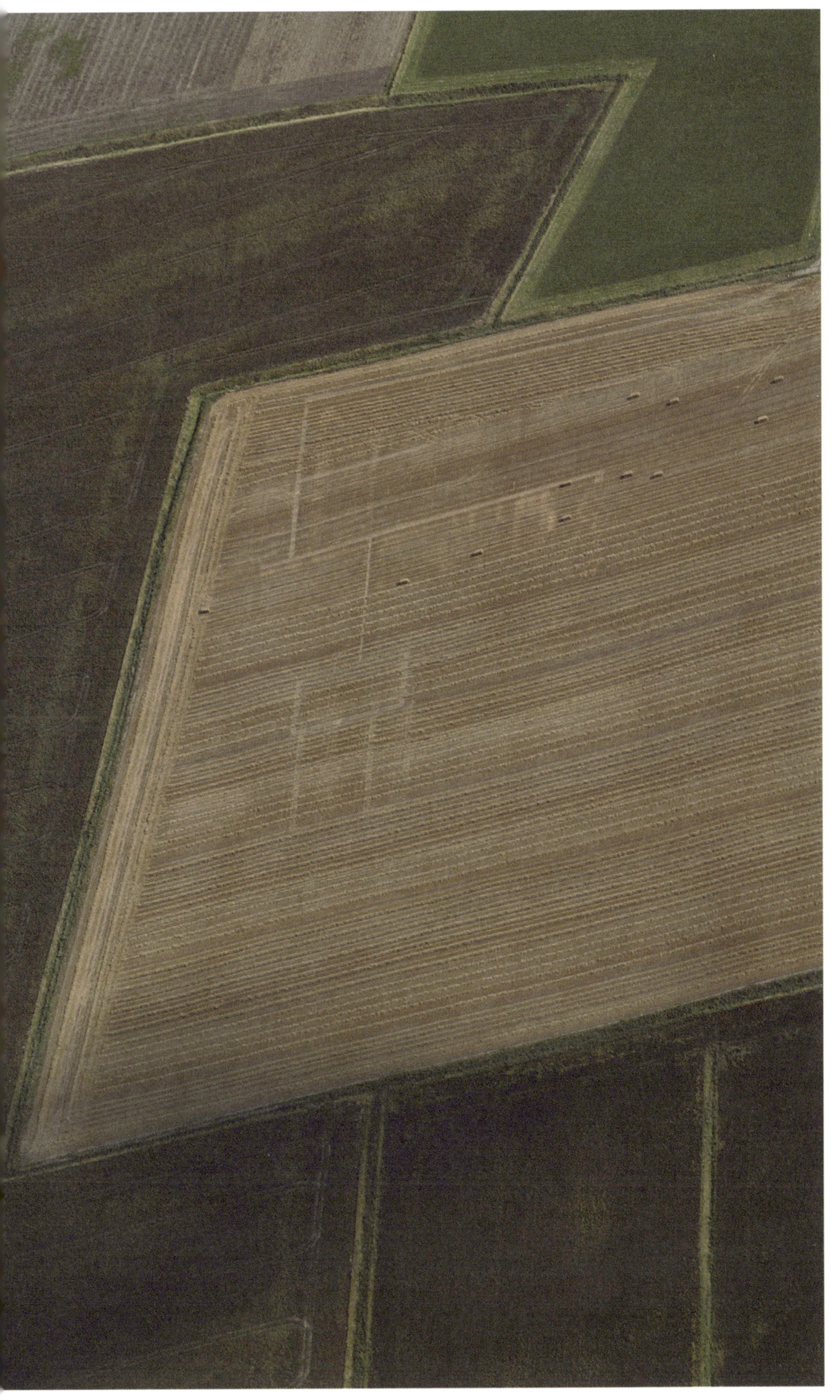

specialists, is unclear. Either way, the medieval reclamations of these fertile silts were used in part to grow crops, in part for grazing sheep and cattle. The area under grass here tended to increase in later centuries, however, so that by 1700 Thomas Cox was able to describe how the farms of the district 'turn to more Profit by Grazing than Ploughing'.

The Fens proper – the areas of peat lying further inland – have a very different history. This was wet, poorly drained land which, until the seventeenth century, was a vast damp common, exploited by communities living around its margins, or on islands within it. The drier areas were grazed for much of the year but the land was primarily valued for the materials which were cut from it: marsh hay, 'litter' for cattle bedding, and reed and sedges, for thatching. Peat for fuel was also extensively excavated, usually from relatively shallow excavations, half a metre to a metre deep, while wildfowl and fish made a useful supplement to the peasant diet. This was a useful landscape to those who lived beside it, as well as being an ecological paradise. Moreover, the rivers, streams and lakes did not serve to divide but to unite: they were important arteries of communication, and the success of towns like Ely or Wisbech was dependent on the navigability of the fen watercourses.

But powerful outsiders viewed this watery landscape differently, as a threat and a challenge. Some limited attempts at drainage, generally restricted to the peat margins, occurred in the medieval period. But it was only in the late sixteenth and early seventeenth centuries that large landowners began to take a serious interest in comprehensive systems of improvement. They wanted to extend the grazing season on the lower peat ground, much of which was under water from autumn until late spring. Some believed that the land could be made dry enough to allow the rich peat soils to be ploughed and cultivated. But many local people were less enthusiastic about the prospect of reclamation. To small farmers, exploiting their rights to use the great wet commons, areas which lay regularly under water might be of real economic importance. As Lord Willoughby pointed out in 1597: 'a poor man may not make more commodity of a fen full of fish, fowl and reed, rented for little or nothing, than of ground made pasture and improved to high rent, as the charges of draining will require, for cattle and kine to feed on'.

In 1585 the General Drainage Act was introduced into Parliament, eventually reaching the statute books in 1600. This established the principle that large landowners could overrule local proprietors and suppress any common rights which obstructed the path of drainage schemes, and that the investors (or 'adventurers') in such schemes might be rewarded with a share of the reclaimed land. Some limited attempts at drainage were made immediately after the passing of the act, and a number of more ambitious schemes, for comprehensive reclamation, were soon mooted. That which eventually went ahead – brought

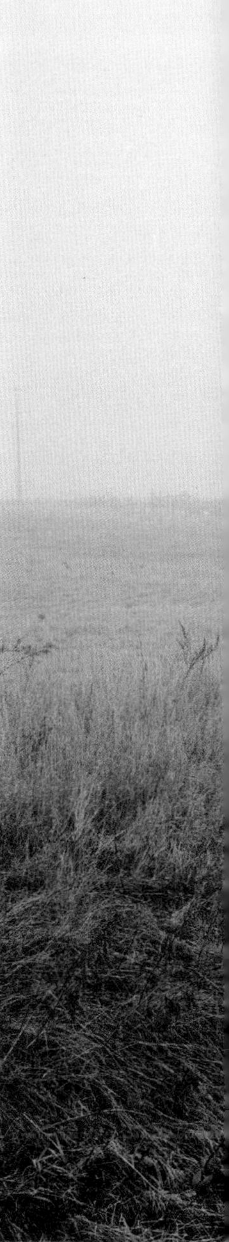

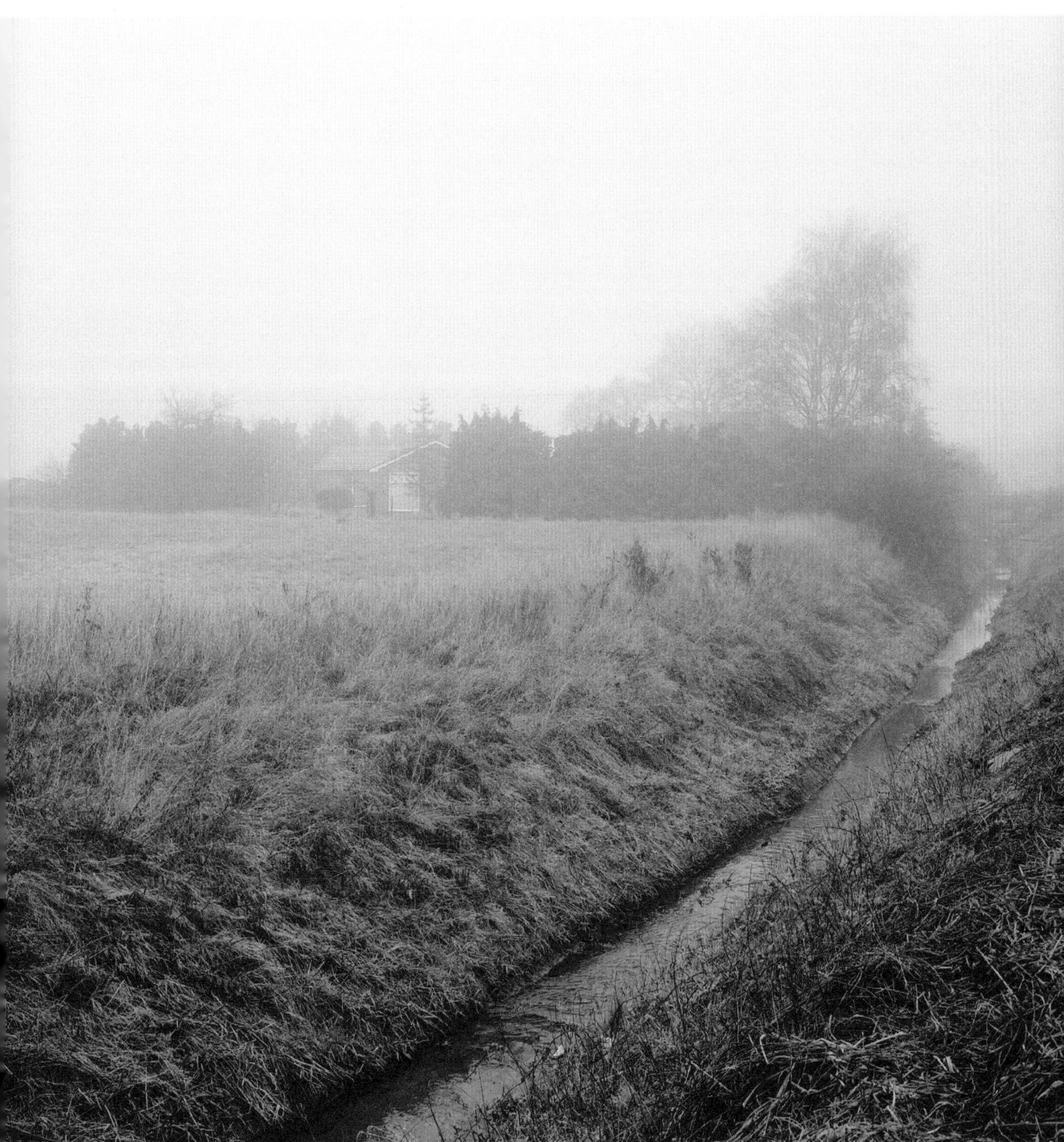

forward by a consortium of investors led by Francis, the Fourth Earl of Bedford –
was directed by a Dutchman, Cornelius Vermuyden. The Dutch were the leading
experts in wetland drainage (much of the land area of their own country
had been reclaimed from the waters) and Dutchmen were advising on land
reclamation schemes throughout Europe at this time. Work on the various
drainage works began in 1634.

Contemporary opinion was divided over the best way of improving drainage
in the Fens. Vermuyden was one of those who believed that the best approach
was to increase the velocity of water flowing down the watercourses, by
straightening them or amalgamating them or both, so as to reduce the risk
of flooding and keep the outfalls to the sea free of sand and shingle. The
principal feature of his scheme was the Seventy Foot or Bedford (later the
'Old Bedford') River: a stupendous piece of engineering that runs dead straight

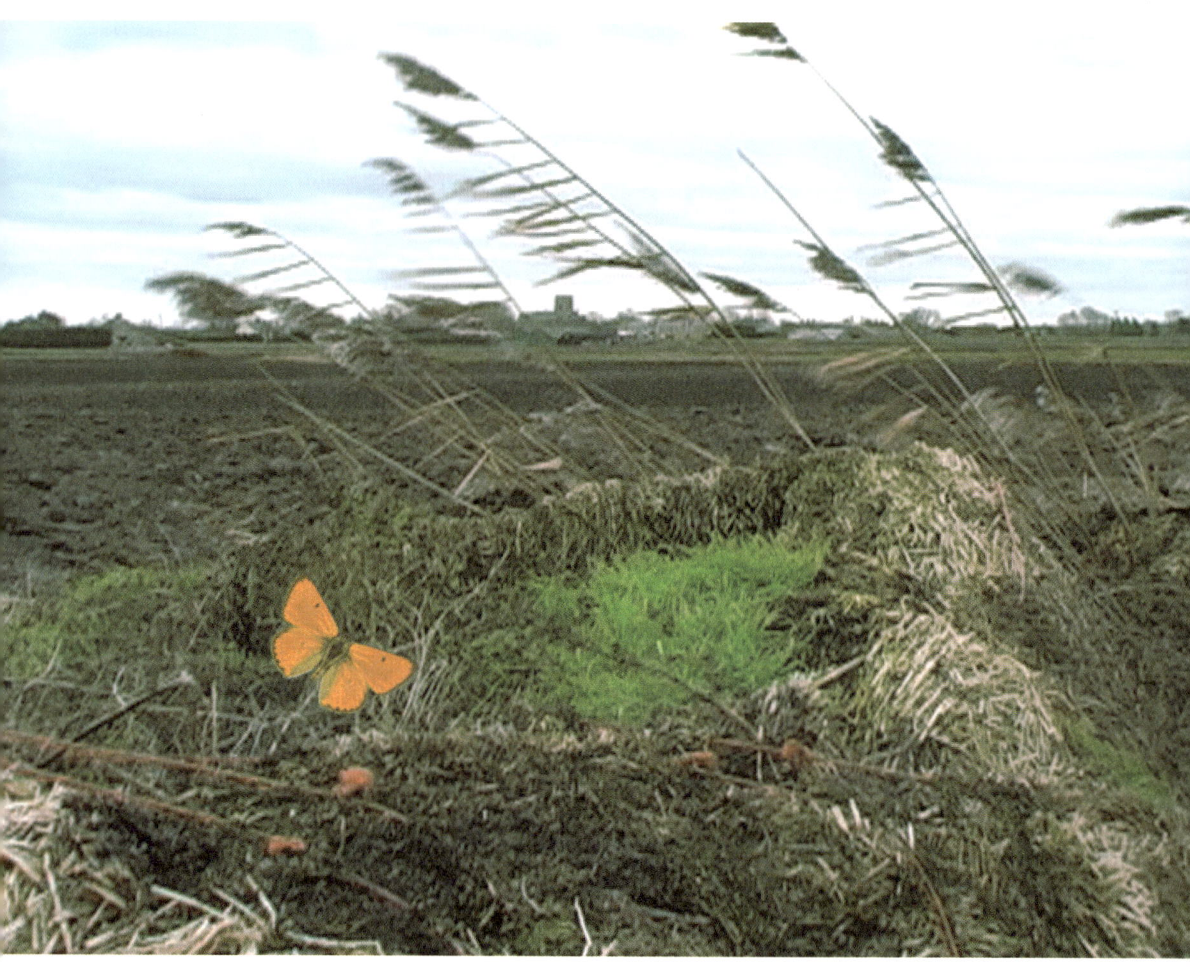

for some 32 kilometres, is 70 feet (c.22 metres) wide, and which served to divert the waters of the meandering river Ouse from Earith, just inside Huntingdonshire, to Denver in Norfolk. There were innumerable smaller dykes, sluices and cut-off channels.

In 1637, at a Session of the Court of Sewers at St Ives, it was declared that the project was completed and that the Great Level was drained. But the new works were only partially successful. There was sustained opposition from the local commoners, involving riots and sabotage. Their objection was less to the drainage works *per se* as to the fact that the allotments made to the 'adventurers' reduced the area of common land available for their use. Large areas continued to be liable to flooding, and in general the situation was deemed unsatisfactory. Charles I therefore appointed a further Commission of Sewers to sit at Huntingdon in 1638, which ruled that the Earl of Bedford and his associates had not fulfilled their obligations. Charles himself took over as director of the scheme and Vermuyden accepted office under him, but the outbreak of the Civil War suspended all further work, and it was only in 1649, with hostilities over and a Republic in place, that attention turned once more to drainage matters.

An Act of Parliament authorised William, Fifth Earl and First Duke of Bedford and his associates to resume drainage work. The stated intention was now to

reclaim the land, not only for improved pasture, but also for arable, and
Vermuyden was once again in charge of operations. His main creation in this
second phase of activity was the Hundred Foot Drain or New Bedford River,
which runs parallel to the Old River. Substantial 'barrier banks' were created on
the outer edges of each, thus creating a vast washland which could store the
waters of the Ouse in time of winter flood. More than 10,000 labourers were
employed on this vast project, which is still awe-inspiring, and so enormous
that it is clearly visible from space. Again, a number of other new watercourses
were created, including the Sixteen Foot or Thurlow's Drain, which runs north
west from Chatteris through Wimblington to the Nene at Upwell, and various
improvements were made to existing watercourses.

In 1653 the works were completed, the Fens were again judged to be
reclaimed, and following the Restoration of the monarchy the 1649 Act, and
the arrangements it put in place, were confirmed by a fresh Act of Parliament.
No less than 95,000 acres were allotted to the 'adventurers' in blocks of land
of various sizes scattered across the Fens. Many can still be picked out on the
modern map as distinct parcels of fields with their drains orientated differently
to those of the surrounding, later enclosures, and bearing the name Adventurers'
Fen, Land, or Grounds (occasionally the name Undertaker's Fen/Lands/Grounds
appears: the 'undertakers' were the contractors who 'undertook' the drainage
work). Some of these dyked fields form patterns which seem to echo the
regular, grid-like arrangements sometimes created by seventeenth-century
drainage of lakes like the Beemster in North Holland, as in the area of Burnt
Fen near Littleport, or at Adventurers' Fen near Haddenham. The seventeenth-
century reclamation of these damp lands was more than a matter of practical
agrarian economics. These were abstract schemes of land division, imposed
on the featureless fen surface, symbolic of the triumph of rational organisa-
tion over the chaos of nature. Indeed, a number of contemporary writers
published much larger and more ambitious schemes of large-scale, system-
atic land division in the Fens, and some even proposed the creation of new
cities here.

Some drainage activity continued into the second half of the seventeenth-
century but this phase of reclamation was effectively completed by the 1660s
and the condition of the Fens was, in agricultural terms, greatly improved.
Although most of the land was still used for grazing some was now ploughed
and planted with crops: there are records of cabbages and cereals being cultivated
on newly reclaimed fen in 1683 at Thorney, while Sir William Dugdale, who
visited Willingham in 1657, reported that onions, peas and hemp were being
grown there. On fen ground to the north east of Ely he saw flax, hemp, oats,
wheat, coleseed and rape, while at Whittlesey fruit trees and extensive cornfields.

But the success of Vermuyden's scheme should not be exaggerated. These kinds of improvements and changes in land use were largely restricted to privately owned land, but only a minority of the Fens was actually *enclosed* at this time — those portions allotted to the undertakers and adventurers, and to some leading local landowners, or divided into private fields by the agreement of the commoners. The majority remained as open common grazing, although it was now often allocated to specific parishes rather than shared between many and, as a result of Vermuyden's drainage works, less liable to serious inundation than before. Some areas still lay entirely unreclaimed. As Dugdale emphasised in 1662, 'there are many great meres and lakes still continuing'. Moreover, at a local level there were many problems with the drainage works, sometimes because of insufficient investment, sometimes because of continuing opposition and sabotage. More importantly, towards the end of the century the condition of the reclaimed lands began to deteriorate. Once water was removed from the absorbent peat it shrank steadily, while on land that was ploughed the peat blew away, and the surface was constantly degraded by microbial action. With remarkable speed the surface of the fields fell below that of the adjacent rivers and channels, and became subject once more to regular flooding. Daniel Defoe described how, crossing the GogMagog Hills near

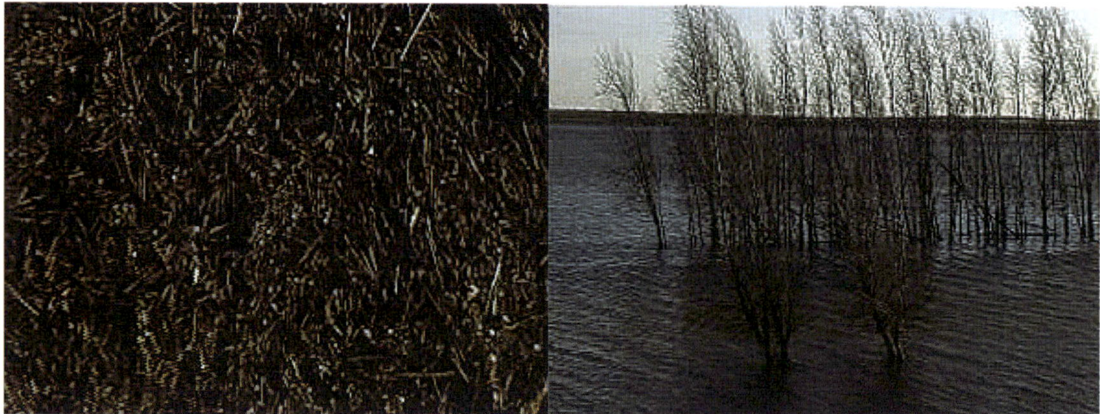

Cambridge shortly before 1720, he saw: 'the Fen country on our right, almost all covered with water like a sea, the Michaelmas rains having been very great this year'. The only solution was to use horse mills or, more usually, drainage windmills, to lift water over the embankments and into the main water courses. From the later seventeenth century, drainage mills became a quintessential feature of the Fen landscape.

The technology of wind drainage was, once again, imported from the Netherlands, where mills were widely established by the fifteenth century. Some were used on the silt fens even in the sixteenth century but it was only

with the drainage and subsequent shrinkage of the peat that they began to be
built on a large scale. Most were simple wooden smock mills with four canvas
sails: they drove 'scoop wheels', which operated rather like a water wheel, but
in reverse, lifting water up from drainage ditches and into a higher-level dyke
or river. Some were erected by individual landowners, some by groups of
neighbours, and some by the various Drainage Commissions – local bodies of
elected landowners who were responsible for drainage works in compact areas
of wetland – established in the course of the eighteenth century. Vast numbers
were built, but the Fens remained poorly drained: the more water was pumped
by the mills, the more the surface shrank, and the higher the water had to be
lifted into the rivers and main drains.

The landscape of the Fens as we know it today was not created in the
seventeenth century, but in the nineteenth. It was in part the product of changes
in land ownership – of the enclosure of the remaining areas of common. This
filled the spaces between the adventurers' allotments, and other early divisions of
the fen commons, with meshes of straight ditches which are generally less grid-
like than those found in the older allotments – long rectangles and attenuated
rhomboids are dominant shapes. But the new landscape was mainly the
product of technological advances – of the employment of steam pumps.
Their use had been mooted by the engineer John Rennie as early as 1803, but
the first engine was only erected, at Sutton St Edmund in Lincolnshire, in 1817.
That at Ten Mile Bank, three miles south of Denver Sluice, was installed in
1819, followed by the engine at Borough Fen in the North Level in 1820, and by
that at Upware in 1821. By the 1850s steam drainage had spread into all parts of
the Fens. The new machines had scoop wheels which were larger, and could
rotate more quickly, than those of windmills, and they could lift more water
through a greater vertical distance. They could also continue to operate whatever the wind conditions. In 1852 JA Clarke estimated that there had once been
around 700 drainage windmills between Cambridge and Lincoln, but the same
area was now served by a mere 17 steam engines which collectively drained
more than 222,000 acres (90,000 hectares). The Duke of Bedford's agent on the
Thorney estate, Tycho Wing, in 1834 described how the new steam engine was
so successful that the eight drainage mills were now redundant. 'I am preparing
to take down and sell as fast as I can dispose of them, the windmills formerly
used for draining on this estate ... it is impossible that they can ever be required
again for the purposes of drainage'. Virtually no trace of wind drainage now
survives in the Fens.

These developments were accompanied by further improvements in the
patterns of major watercourses, including the construction of the Eau Brink Cut
in 1821, the Ouse Cut between Ely and Littleport in 1827, the North Level Main
Drain between 1831 and 1834, and the new outfall to the Nene in the late 1820s.

All this investment and effort was amply rewarded by a phenomenal expansion of arable farming. By the late 1830s more than half the area of the peat fens was under cultivation and in 1836 George Calthrop, a corn merchant, could insist before a government inquiry that the price of wheat in England was being adversely effected by the 'immense tracts of land brought into cultivation in the Fens of Lincolnshire, Cambridgeshire and Norfolk'. Nor did improvement stop there. In the course of Victoria's reign the last remaining areas of open water and wet fen were enclosed and drained, including Grunty Fen in Cambridgeshire in 1857 and Holme Fen in Huntingdonshire in 1848. The fen surface continued to shrink and erode: an iron column seven metres long was hammered into the fen surface at the latter place immediately after drainage began, and within twelve years, two metres were exposed; by 1890, three metres. There were further refinements in drainage technology with the use, from the 1840s, of light 'grasshopper' engines, and from the 1850s of centrifugal (or turbine) pumps. By the 1870s, around 75 per cent of the peat soils were under the plough.

The pride of contemporary engineers in their achievement is neatly encapsulated in the plaque affixed to the gable of the engine house built in 1830 beside the New Bedford River for the Littleport and Downham Drainage Commissioners:

These Fens have oft times been by Water drown'd.
Science a remedy in Water found.
The powers of Steam she said shall be employ'd
And the Destroyer by Itself destroy'd.

Such pride was justified: this was the most productive arable land in England, producing wheat yields far in excess of any other district. Potatoes too were cultivated and – as an added bonus – the improvements in drainage reduced the number of mosquitoes and thus, by the end of the century, ensured the effective disappearance of malaria.

The reclamation of the peat fens was thus a more protracted and a more complex process than is sometimes assumed, and as a consequence the landscape itself is more varied and intricate than appears at first sight, with numerous different blocks of dyked fields orientated in different directions. Some represent enclosures of fen ground dating to before the great schemes of Vermuyden; others are allotments given to adventurers, undertakers and wealthy landowners in the seventeenth century; most represent portions of fen ground which were only enclosed and divided in the eighteenth and nineteenth centuries. Farms are scattered across them, erected soon after enclosure, and usually occupying the long, low ridges called 'roddons' - silt

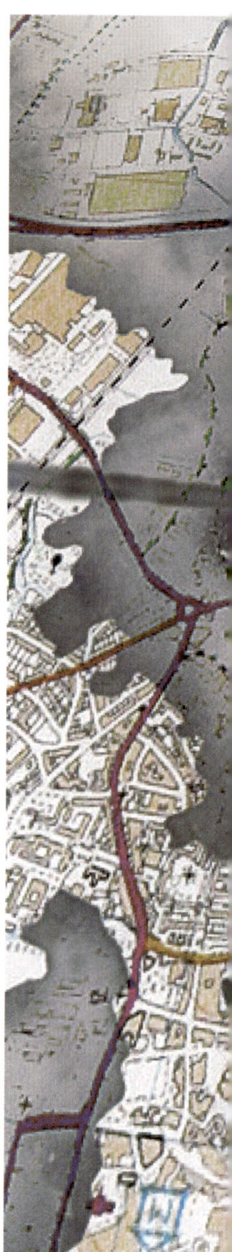

Annabel Howland still from animation *Cut Drains, Charts, Creeks and Cuts*

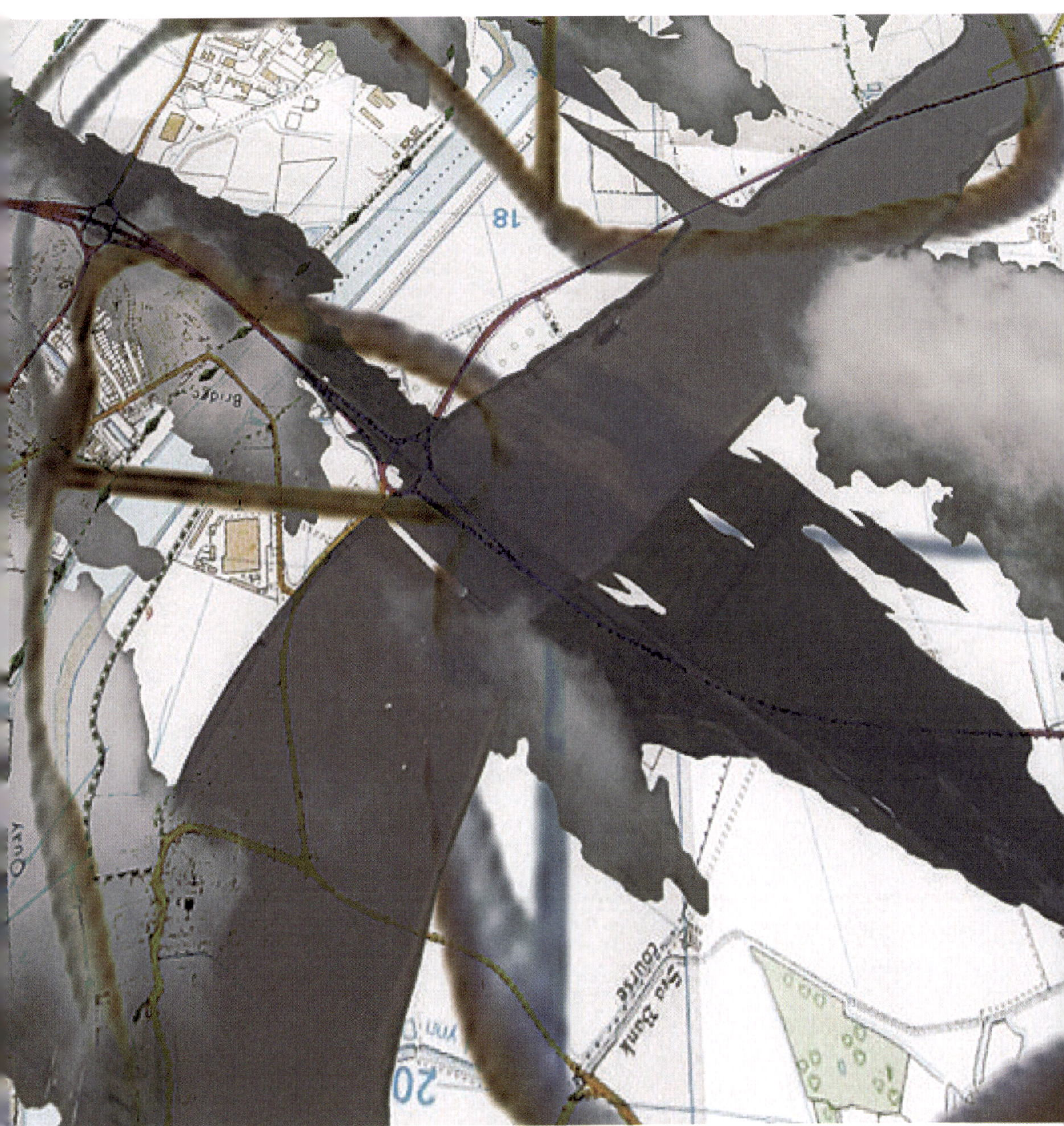

and gravel beds of lost rivers, now standing proud of the shrinking peat. The
long and complex story of reclamation, the fact that the fen ground was carefully
carved up, in stages, in surveyed and measured parcels, coupled with the ruler-
straight character of many of the artificial watercourses created by successive
generations of drainage engineers, has ensured that this is, above all, a highly
rectilinear landscape, and one in which both major and minor roads repeatedly
go round ninety-degree bends. As Dorothy L Sayers' fictional Lord Wimsey
commented on a visit to the Fens: 'I do wish everything wasn't so rectangular
in this part of the world'. It is a strange landscape, and above all a practical and
functional one. But it is also one with a fascinating history, which can still be
read in the layout of its roads, dykes, banks and drains.

Simon Willmoth Why were you interested in working on a commission for the *Silicon Fen* project? What were the particular themes or elements that attracted you? How did your involvement come about?

Suky Best I was approached out of the blue about the commission and was very pleased to be asked to submit a proposal. I was interested in the commission, as I try to find projects that involve my working in rural areas. I had also just finished making a series of animations where I had filmed real insects for research. This led to my meeting many ecologists, so the things they had said to me about plummeting insect populations were in my mind when I went to visit the Fens to write the *Silicon Fen* proposal. A friend of mine mentioned Wicken Fen as being a lovely place to visit, so I planned a weekend where I would go there to try to get a sense of the place. Wicken Fen is beautiful but when you're there you're very conscious that it's an island in the middle of a sea of agri-industry. The following day I went for a long walk around March and Manea, a typical Fenland walk. It was a grey day at the beginning of November. There seemed to be no wildlife, no hedges, few trees; it was a bleak and desolate place. What struck me most was the lack of flies or insects. On returning home I did some research and found that insect and wildlife populations had fallen in this area and that Wicken Fen was an island of biodiversity but like all islands it had problems supporting diversity. Further research revealed that the problems of diminishing diversity and population decline in wildlife was what I wanted to make work about.

TNWK TNWK was wholly based in East Anglia at that time. We had often discussed issues of geographical and demographical and historical particularity, especially in and around those areas between Cambridge, Lowestoft and Norwich, which we had frequented between us over many years. The subject of the commission, as articulated in the invitation, and its formulation as a project was intriguing to us.

Susan Collins *Fenlandia* was a collision of a number of thoughts and processes. Initially it came out of another work altogether. I was making the work *Transporting Skies* (2002), which quite literally was transporting the sky, swapping it (and re-projecting it) between Newlyn Art Gallery in Cornwall and Site Gallery in Sheffield. I was keen to make a second piece, which could locate the work visually more specifically to Sheffield and Newlyn.

I took as my starting point the fact that the first transatlantic Morse code message was transmitted by Marconi from Cornwall, and given that I had very little bandwidth left to play with I tried to work out how I might be able to transmit an image by Morse, how long it would take and what it might look like. What emerged were my first pixel landscapes. Collected pixel by pixel horizontally from top left to bottom right of the screen, and continually writing over themselves when 'complete', the images were transmitted – and updated – live to the gallery in the opposite

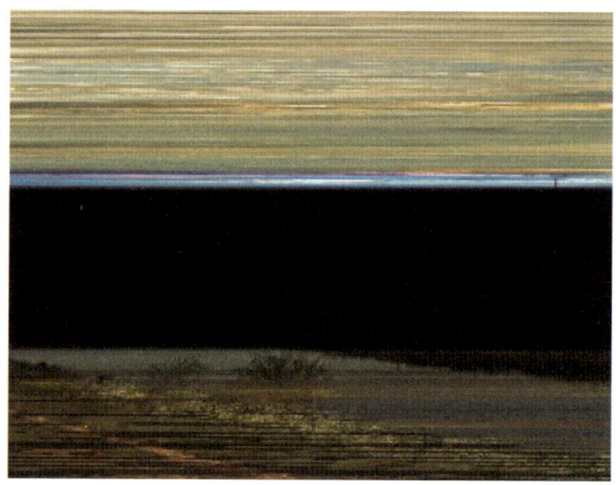

Susan Collins *Fenlandia*

location for the duration of the exhibition.

A few months later I met with Steven Bode (Film and Video Umbrella) who was commissioning online work for *Silicon Fen*. What drew me to the project was the focus on the relationship between landscape and technological innovation in the region where not only are there clusters of new technology companies but that the technology is literally embedded in the flat horizons of a reclaimed landscape of canals, sluices, dykes and ditches. It seemed the perfect opportunity not only to marry the horizontality of my pixel land-scapes to their subject, but also to develop the work further, distributing it live online as well as having the opportunity to archive, or harvest, images from the work over the course of a full year.

Dalziel + Scullion As artists we are always keen to work on a project when there are good people to work with. We felt the partnership of Norwich School of Art and Design and Film and Video Umbrella had a great amount of experience in both the subject matter of the project and the technical expertise to help produce something exciting and ambitious.

Our work looks at how mankind as a species interacts with the various landscapes we inhabit so the Fens project was of great interest providing us with an opportunity to look at a different set of habitats and interactions.

Stephen Hughes I was interested in the commission on a number of levels. The theme of manmade and technological intervention on a once natural landscape fitted well within the broader context of my photography. I saw the project as a natural extension of my existing practice. Also, having read JG Ballard's *Supercannes* I became interested in attempting to photograph the topography and atmospheres of hi-tech business parks. I had briefly visited and

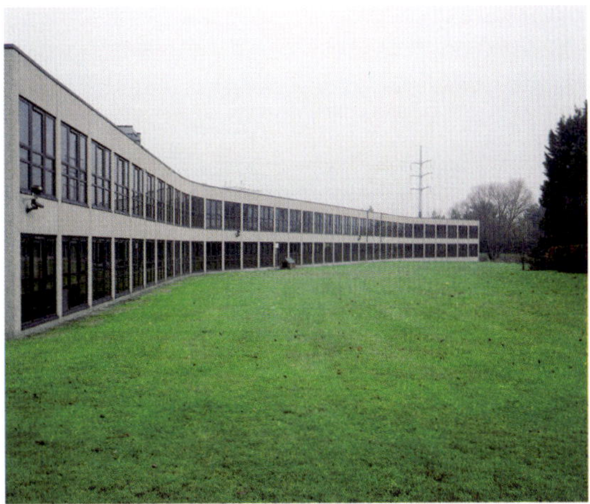

photographed some of these parks in France but *Silicon Fen* gave me the opportunity to investigate these places further. Lastly, having spent the previous five years working predominantly overseas I welcomed the challenge of taking photographs in the UK again, in a landscape I was quite familiar with.

Annabel Howland I was approached by Steven Bode of Film and Video Umbrella for *Silicon Fen* towards the end of 2004. He had seen my work in the catalogue for *Landscape Trauma in the age of scopophilia*, which was curated by Richard Hylton in 2001. For *Landscape Trauma...* I developed work from photographs I had taken while flying over and driving through the mid-west and western USA.

In the triptych *Cut Aerials (USA) 1-3 (2001)* I made for *Landscape Trauma...* I cut the land away from aerial photographs of Arizona, Nevada, and Southern Utah, where dry land, rivers and lakebeds are punctuated with clusters of square and circular fields which are sustained by pumping water from underground. In this arid environment, these perfectly geometric, sometimes brown, some-times lurid green discs seem to hover slightly, like alien presences.

I initially embarked on editing photographs by cutting as a way to feel out the limits of representation, to interrogate the authority of the photographic and, more recently, the cartographic image, and to open up other potential narrative structures, meanings or etymologies. At the time

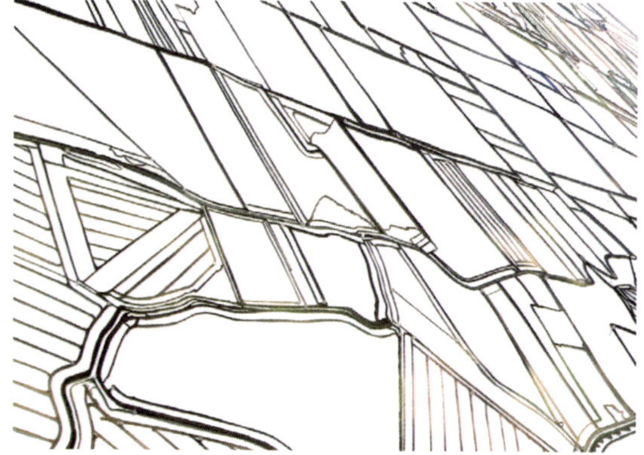

I was interested in the relationship between the image and death:

> *...In the rare instances when a living person shows similitude with himself, he only seems to us more remote, closer to a dangerous neutral region, astray in himself and like his own ghost already: he seems to return, no longer having any but an echo of life. [...]The fixed image knows no repose, and this is above all because it poses nothing, establishes nothing. Its fixity, like that of the corpse, is the position of what stays with us because it has no place.*
> Maurice Blanchot, *The Space of Literature.*

SW How did the themes of Silicon Fen relate to your previous work?

SC The majority of my work has been made in response to different sites and situations. Some of the work is situated in public spaces, some in galleries, some online and some distributed across all three. Whilst working directly with the British landscape is something relatively recent in the work, exploring the collision between the real and the virtual (or artificial) and working with networks and remote transmission as primary materials have been ongoing preoccupations.

The *Silicon Fen* project has offered an opportunity to not only encode a landscape image over time, inscribing it and reinscribing it each day, but also to consider what it means materially to record a digital image and transmit it across space and time. In developing the work a parallel has emerged between the material of the image made up of individual pixels of transmitted time, and the manmade, technologically embedded landscape. *Fenlandia* represents what in this technological day and age appears to be an almost perverse desire to slow things down. More a space for contemplation than participation, *Fenlandia* provides a live – if remote – window on the landscape to an international online audience.

I find it interesting, and exciting, that what in many senses is such a cool, mechanistic process can produce such evocative and often stirring images. I view these pixel landscapes as a kind of 'open system'. I have made works that I have thought of as open systems before, such as *In Conversation* (1997-2001), which required the viewers to inhabit and activate the work for it to exist. Here, however, the system is instead inhabited and activated by light, day, night, weather, movement of the sun, the seasons and all these variables that conspire to produce an infinite variety of unique images. In some respects this would appear to make the work less 'corruptible' by humans/viewers than my earlier 'interactive' experiments where the potential for variable content was broad, but the actual range of user interaction would tend to be quite limited and often banal. Having said that there are human

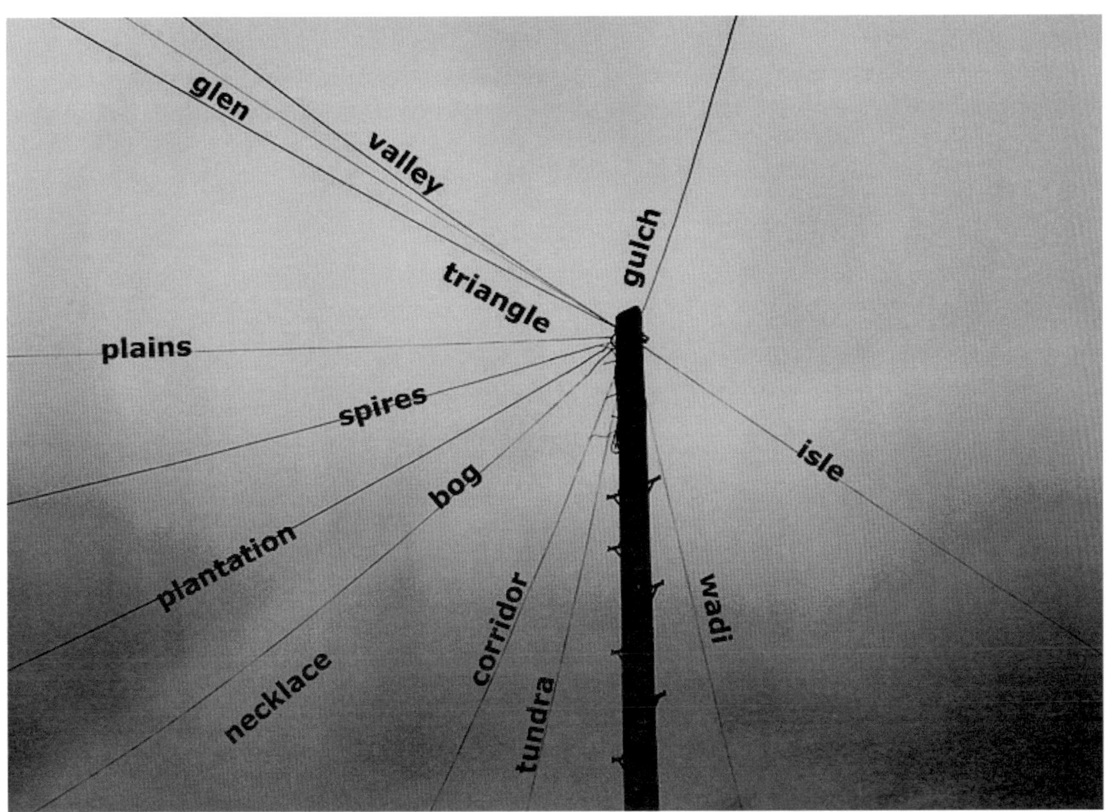

interventions (beyond stray pixel appearances), which make themselves visible in the work. On 20th December 2004 in the Anchor Inn version of *Fenlandia*, the tree to the left of the image disappeared from view. At first I thought the camera had moved in strong winds, however all the other markers, such as the telegraph pole, were still in the same position. I found out later that the tree had been chopped down because of subsidence and all the Anchor Inn *Fenlandia* images thereafter have a bleaker, more abstract and less arcadian feel to them.

TNWK We are interested in notions of 'the commons' and in a portraiture of shared values. Previous work such as *Millennium Collection* (2000) had performed functions akin to that which was called 'the conversation piece' in the eighteenth century; through an interface between analogue materiality (in the case of the 'collection' the handling actual objects and their histories) and digital representations of those 'occurrences'. We were keen to see what might happen when our interest in the temporal, the located and the specific was brought into a productive tension between analogue and digital representations of a largely abstract concept such as *Silicon Fen*.

TNWK set out to explore the idea of the term 'Silicon Fen', with a view to the value of its coinage for those who lived or worked within its notional analogue and digital territories. We were interested in networks, communities 'on' the land and communities 'off' the land, for whom the term 'Silicon Fen' might have any valency. We researched, we conversed, we engaged others in conversation.

TNWK works through largely synchronous collaboration. We share all of the decision-making and consequently most of the making. In such a process there remain subtleties of inflection around which hand is making a particular mark at a specific time; this might be to do with pushing the shutter on a camera or a configuration of notes on a page or the drift of a conversation with a potential further partner, but it also concerns mouse-control, who happens to have their hand on the mouse at a given moment. We try to remain conscious of difficulties, in terms of responsibility for particular moments, that might arise from those subtleties.

AH Several of the key themes of the project and the region related to landscape-based work I was already doing and offered the opportunity to pursue these interests in more depth in relation to a specific, limited area. Rather than making an optical evaluation of a region's surface, charting the marks of geological, meteorological and human intervention, *Silicon Fen* offered me the possibility of scratching beneath the surface and looking at a wider range of relationships and features that have formed this area's appearance, use and representation. In the title of a piece I made for Mois de la Photo in Montreal in 1999 (*Up-and-Downways versus Longways*) I referred to the view of roads held by Anse in William Faulkner's *As I Lay Dying*. Anse sees the arrival of the road and the changes it brings to his environment and the people around him as the source of all his woes:

*When He aims for something to be always
a-moving, He makes it long ways, like a road
or a horse or a wagon, but when He aims for
something to stay put, He makes it up-and-
down ways, like a tree or a man... if He'd*

*aimed for man to be always a-moving and
going somewheres else, wouldn't He a put
him longways on his belly, like a snake?*
William Faulkner, *As I Lay Dying*

You can imagine the Fenlanders of the seventeenth-century regarding with similar suspicion the dikes, drains and cuts outsiders began to dig into their soggy land. Each phase of their history has brought major physiological change to the Fens and these changes remain largely visible. Ice-age transitions between freeze and thaw left scars in the land; the development of early agriculture to the west of the region dislodged sand and soil which flowed down-stream silting up the waterways of the Fens, causing them to flood; various phases of draining, flooding and road building followed by rail and airfield construction. The residue is an intricate network of lines and contours across the land, each layer of which points to a shift in the inhabitants' and users' orientation to location, transit, communication and elsewhere. The latest phase in this spread of arteries is the electronic and radio network of cables and channels invisibly interlacing across the region in twenty-first century channels of communication.

An important feature of much of my work of the last few years has been the alteration of the viewer's physical and cognitive orientation to the image. The translations through reproduction, enlargement, cutting and reconfiguration to which I subject the photographic or cartographic image explore relations between site and sight and generate new spatial and temporal effects. This brings the images to a point where they oscillate between being fragile, skeletal remains and strong physical and visual presences. The way representation in my work frequently teeters between coherence and collapse seemed to correspond with the Fens' precarious existence between flooding, drying out, or wearing thin.

D+S In previous works like *The Pressure of Spring* (1999) and *Storm* (2003) we examined two very different types of habitat; the first was on the north east coast of Scotland and was a manipulated, industrialised and peopled landscape. This land-scape was engineered to provide the basic staples for a large urban population and housed a gas powered energy plant, military communication bases, extensive arable and livestock agriculture land uses, and the two largest white fish ports in Europe. Within this coastal landscape the power of the sea and the elements were always present. In the second work, *Storm*, we looked at a different set of habitats, this time across the highlands of Scotland where the shape of the landscape had changed at a much slower pace and for entirely different reasons – this landscape, shaped by glaciers and erosion, was very scarcely populated. So the *Silicon Fen* project offered us the opportunity to examine a landscape, which was in contrast to the landscapes we were familiar with and added to our knowledge of landscape and our portfolio of works.

SB The themes of *Silicon Fen* related to the insect animations that I completed in 2005. I was examining and remaking movements of groups of insects, then making abstract animations derived from these movements in order to create a hypnotic state. The works were placed in clinical areas of hospitals where patients were experiencing high levels of stress. This led to my spending a lot of time with the ecologists at London's wetland centre and at Slimbridge. Whilst talking about insect populations with the ecologists I discovered that they were extremely concerned about insect populations and couldn't discover the causes for their fluctuations and that no one else was interested. Rather than insects it was animals

further up the food chain that caught the public's imagination. I had studied geography for my first degree and ecology was a part of this. It was frightening that the doomsday predictions about climate change, habitat loss and the impact of modern farming practices were all coming true 25 years later. In 1982 I had been on a geography field trip to the Fens, where we examined the possible impact that the increases in field size would have on soil quality, quantity, increased winds speeds and the diversity of animal populations. It was bleak to see all the predictions made then coming true.

SW How did you interpret the project brief for the commission in the work you produced, what research did you do?

AH I decided to approach the brief from as many different angles as possible and keep an open mind about how the work would develop and what kind of work might emerge. One of the things that most struck me about the Fens when I first looked at them closely on an Ordnance Survey map was the number of names that are measurements: Hundred Foot Washes, Twenty Foot River, Forty Foot Drain. For my first trip in February the route I plotted through the Fens took me around as many of these 'measured' places as possible, through sun, rain, hail and snow. On the next trips in early July and late August I flew and drove around the Fens photo-graphing them from the air and the ground. I spaced my trips to ensure seeing the region in as many different seasons as possible. I met with several farmers who were able to fill in agricultural details and historical and anecdotal facts, and I met with a former chairman of one of the Fens' Internal Drainage Boards, who gave me a lot of information about the history of the drainage of the Fens and the precarious position they are now in.

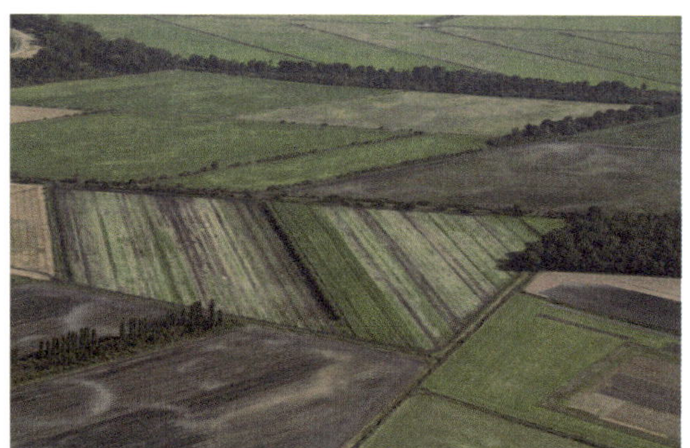

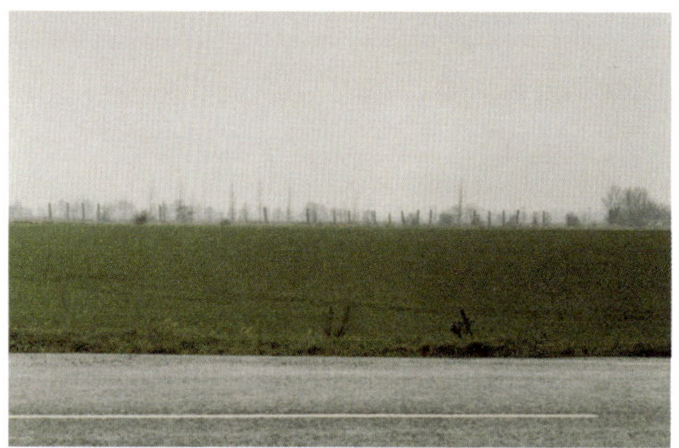

The more information and images I gathered, the more it became apparent to me that I didn't want to just make photographic work in response to the project, not only because this would mean discarding a large amount of interesting material, but also because I wanted my contribution to link in more directly with the framework of the *Silicon Fen* project as a whole. I therefore settled on four different kinds of work: cut-outs, photographs, 3-D animation and a website.

For the cut-outs, I selected three aerial shots of areas that exemplified the terrain: Hundred Foot Washes, Gedney Drove End and Green Dike. As in earlier work, I cut away the land from the image leaving behind the marks of the networks of waterways and roads which reveal the intensity of human intervention. *Blizzard Fen* and *Fenscope 1 & 2* are taken from the ground and focus on the way the flatness of the Fens makes everything

appear in relation to a vanishing point or horizon; the verticals of telegraph poles and trees fasten the lines that traverse the foregrounds to the voids of grey skies above the horizons. On the other hand, the series of photographs taken from the air focus on the palimpsestic qualities of the land, revealing intricate patterns left by geological and agricultural change and use. The nice thing about showing this work locally was that at each exhibition I learnt more about what I had photographed from the people who came. The many farmers who came to the opening at King's Lynn filled me in on agricultural details and a geologist working at Babylon Gallery in Ely was able to identify or confirm the identities of certain geological features in some of the other images (e.g. roddons, extinct river courses surviving as light-coloured silt; remnants of pingos – dome-shaped mounds consisting of a layer of soil over a large core of ice – which survive as light, circular forms in the soil). Much of this information was added to the website which came to be called Howworld (I found a How Fen, my name is Howland, so the site became Howworld).

Howworld.com is composed of photographic and cartographic montages, animation, images, vocabulary and particularly resonant names. It also presents different views and representations of a strange, flying-saucer-like island I spotted just off the coast in the Wash. This flawlessly circular form turned out to have a number of identities and to be described or located differently in the maps I looked at: sometimes there were two islands, though I only saw one. It turned out to be a practice bombing target, possibly a trial freshwater lagoon; I also heard it had been built to accommodate the first radar in the Second World War. Its perfectly round form and unexpected emergence between the clouds as I flew along the coast reminded me of the circular fields in the US. Interestingly, both areas are intensively used by the military.

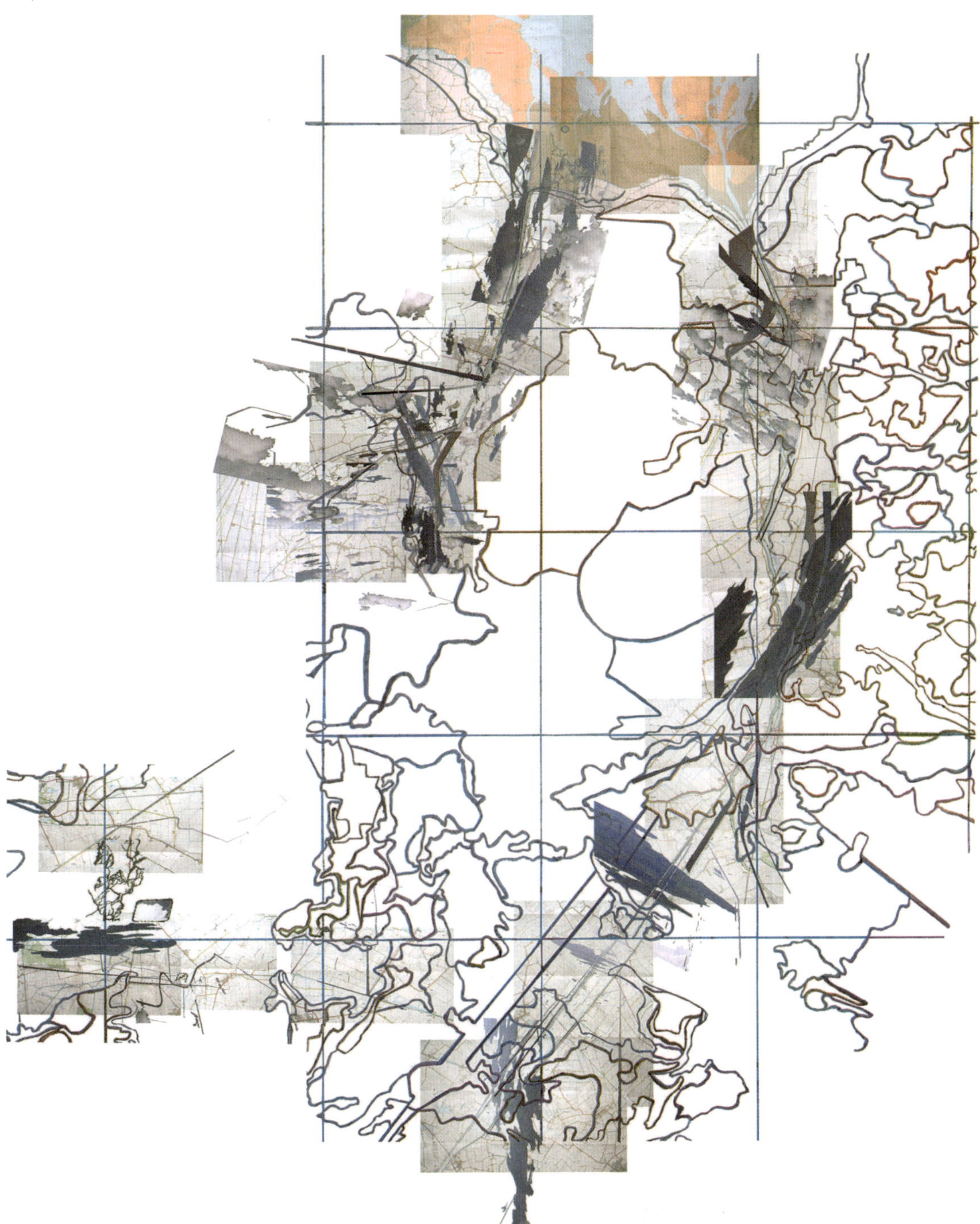

I chose the title of the show, *Drains, Cables, and Cuts* to reflect features that mark and transect the Fens, how my work is made, and the prosaic character of fen names. For my digital animation, *Cut Drains, Charts, Creeks and Cuts* I cut out aerial photographs of the Fens so that only watercourses, clouds and the shadows of clouds remain. These fragile images were then matched to their corresponding locations on a map, which had also been heavily edited so that the only numbers and words relating to water remain visible. The overlaying of cut-out photographs, each of which had different viewpoints and was shot at a different angle, meant that although each photographic element converged perfectly with the map at one point at least, they also diverged drastically from the map at other points. This montage of edited photos and map was further overlaid with brightly coloured contours derived from a soil chart of the area. This composite image was then animated into a 3-D 'fly-through' travelling along key Fenland waterways, down adjoining cuts and creeks, beginning and ending in The Wash. The title plays on 'cut' as a verb and a noun, while its repetition at the beginning and end reflects the loop 'flown' in the film. Maintaining the prosaic tone, the title also simply lists key elements and acts inherent in the region and the work.

D+S In the work for *Silicon Fen*, *Earthdom*, our interest in the interconnectedness of life extends to our own human role within this — of the synthesis between biology and ideas, the tangible links between industrial and social advancements and the inevitable impact of these on local and global environments. For human consciousness to exist at all on earth it must be sustained and nourished by a staggering array and continual flow of substances. Amidst the complex levels of zinc and iron, magnesium and calcium is water, an apparently benign yet crucial substance that finds its way into every minuscule part of us and into every other form of organic life. Contemporary landscapes are now criss-crossed with a network of often-invisible conduits of water/energy/

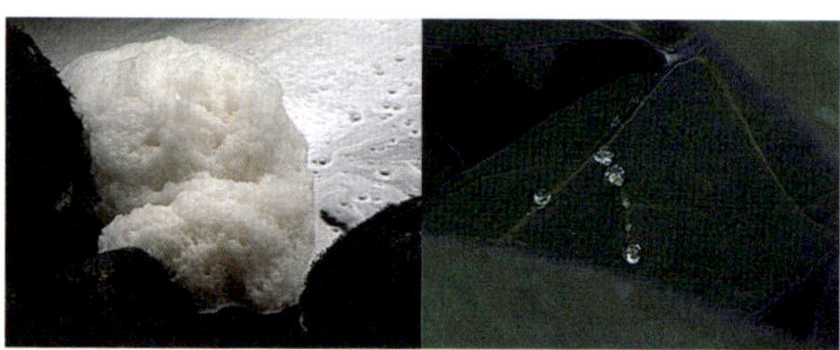

communication and in this work we explored the notion of the interventions of mankind as being part of the rhythms of the landscape — through

which water, blood and electricity flow as complex and interconnected systems, In *Earthdom* we tried to find new metaphors to interpret the carousel of activity and interdependent relationships that are present in the contemporary landscape. The music that accompanies the work combines two tracks by Japanese sound artists Ryoji Ikeda and Akio Suzuki. We have long admired their work and felt that the mood of these pieces would work well with the film — and were able to contact them and gain permission to use the various pieces in the project.

SH I knew I wanted to visit the science parks around Cambridge and Ely but apart from that I was happy to keep an open mind about the project until I saw the Fens. The first thing that struck me was the almost complete absence of people in the science parks, out in the agricultural

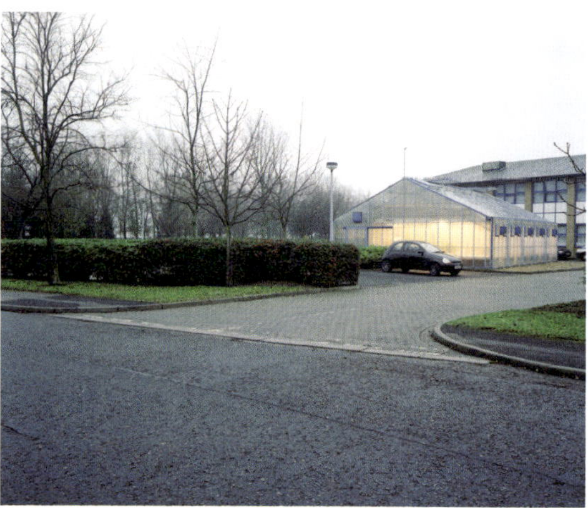

areas and alongside the cuts and waterways. This landscape, empty of people, but one that has been so intensively marked, managed and manoeuvred, was intriguing. The lines made by the agricultural planting, channels and phone wires along with the marks left by the various machines became important to the work. The science parks seemed completely at home in the Fens. Their empty and lost atmosphere seemed to mirror that of the fields. I tried to show this in the photographs. After discussions with Film and Video Umbrella we decided to split the photographs into two folios. This was a presentational device for the website. I wanted to mix up the photographs of the science parks within those of the Fens, as opposed to creating two distinct groups. I always try to avoid presenting my work in typologies. I like a more open approach.

SB I interpreted the brief to fit my own ideas around wildlife loss. I decided to use digital technology to make the work, not for this to be the subject of the work. After my visit to the Fens I decided that the works had to be about the lack of wildlife. I decided to use museum specimens of insects, birds and animals and re-animate them into contemporary Fenland settings to highlight the crisis in diminishing wildlife and play upon the concepts of animation and re animation. The title of the piece described the work, referencing Thomas Hardy's novel *The Return of the Native*, which is about doomed relationships after a man returns to his village after a successful career abroad. I wanted there to be some impossibility of success in returning the species to their native places. The insects and animals were photographed from the Victorian natural history collection at Bedford Museum, many collected from the Fens, so to digitally return them to their habitat added poignancy to the work. The animations were made with winter landscapes, again to add to the impossibility of the work being real in any way. The animations were made to look convincing but not too real. I wanted them to look good but knew that they couldn't possibly compete with contemporary CGI effects so I deliberate left a slightly 'clunky' crudeness to them. The insect sounds were all

taken from the British Library; again the source was important, that the sounds were held for posterity by a major institution. The animations were made small so as to allude to vitrines in natural history displays. I made a series of prints to increase the number of insects and animals shown. This was to emphasise the lack of variety of wildlife in the contemporary Fenland landscape. The prints benefited from the wind and other sounds that overlapped from the animations in the exhibition. One of the major aspects of the work was the titles, which had to be factual and scientifically correct. The titles being about each species and the location of the image would bring a tension to the obvious fictions being depicted. As long as the titles were correct I could be fanciful and ridiculous in the images.

Liz Robin did all the research for me and we would discuss areas that I was interested in and

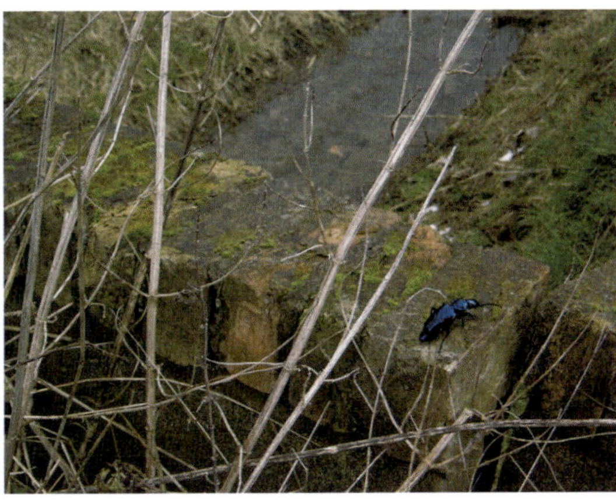

types of animals and she would go and gather data. I think that without her I couldn't have made this piece, and the research really led the resultant works. We were also really lucky with Chris Andrew at Bedford Museum. He looks after the natural history collection and gave us fantastic access to all their specimens and is also a very enthusiastic and knowledgeable person.

TNWK We gathered photos, we drove the roads and walked the land. We gathered extensive notes. We did interviews. We attended the Straw Bear Festival in Whittlesey. We even went ten-pin bowling with some computer programmers who were directly employed to work for companies based in 'Silicon Fen'. We used photography, video, notebooks, field recordings.

We also did web trawls, we used a search-engine orientated poetics modality for text-generation known as 'flarf'. Flarf is a bricolage text-generation method that employs internet search engines. For example: you search Google for two disparate terms like 'silicon' and 'fen', then, using the quotes captured you stitch words phrases, clauses and sentences together to assemble new texts. We're interested in the conversation between the process of editing implied by this approach and the activity of reclaiming land. Flarf has so far been interesting for a number of reasons – its collaborative texture, its anthropological implications (the sampling of an enormous variety of public speech based on a common word or phrase shared) and its comedic potential for critique.

The title *far from silicon fen* indicates a sense of imprecision as to exactly 'where' is being re-ferred to, in terms of the place 'Silicon Fen', and that imprecision directly emerged from our ex-perience trying to locate the term not simply within the geographical area but as a slippery term with which those on the ground, in that geographical area, were in any meaningful way familiar. We went looking, initially, for acknowledgment that 'Silicon Fen' registered as a place for those held to live and work within its territorial bounds; we found far more acknowledgment on the internet than among the farm-hands, heritage wardens, shopkeepers, millers, publicans and day-trippers with whom we made contact. *far from silicon fen* also clearly

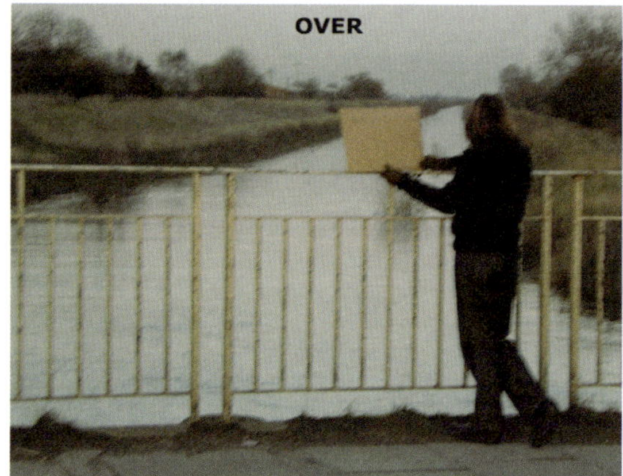

suggests distance; in particular that distance which could be achieved through technological remove, setting into motion a kind of awkward misfit between materials in differing realms. This titling also sets up play with the vernacular sense of 'far from it' as a phrase that indicates that something is not true.

SC The timescale of the project gave me a unique opportunity to develop a piece (and series) of work over time. The ongoing engagement with the locations (each reliant on remote locations and the goodwill and infrastructure of hosts) allowed the work to evolve and develop in a way that is not usually possible. The research trips were spent driving around the Fens looking for potential vantage points. My primary focus was the rural location; however, in keeping with the *Silicon Fen* project I was looking for a pair of locations, one rural and one technological.

For the rural location I was looking for an image that would be able to encapsulate a sense of the fen landscape whilst pictorially referencing a landscape tradition. A combination of trees, sky, fields and water were key elements. However, what was also essential was the potential to be connected to electricity and the internet, and a secure place for the camera.

My first research trip was in December 2003. I looked for a place to stay overnight that was in the countryside, and found the Anchor Inn at Sutton Gault, a 17th century coaching inn over-looking the Great Ouse and the New Bedford River. Immediately it seemed like a very possible location for the camera. The view from the bedroom window was very close to the images I had been imagining. However, this was at the very start of my search and part of me had also been interested in the possibility of siting the camera on a bridge looking directly down a drain, so I continued exploring, driving up and down just about all the drains in the region looking for possible vantage points without success. All roads led back to the Anchor Inn and just a few weeks before the project was due to launch the proprietor very generously agreed to house the first *Fenlandia* camera on the roof.

During this period I was also driving around technology parks looking for a suitable technological 'partner' location, eventually to be Cambourne Business Park with its own manmade mini Fenland water feature landscaped into it. Whilst driving around these parks what struck me most were the names of the companies — all sounded either randomly generated or genetically

modified. This idealised technology park language inspired, in part, the title of the work, *Fenlandia*.

SW What was your experience of the Fens as a landscape and as a place?

D+S Our familiarity with Scotland, where hills are somehow always present, made the flatness of the Fen landscape seem quite alien. Its open and expansive qualities made us feel exposed, anything sited or moving upon this landscape becomes very noticeable. Yet it was perhaps the light and great skyscapes that this flat landscape afforded that made the strongest impression.

SB I was in the Fens in January, February and March of 2005. It was a bleak, cold time of year to be there and I'm sure that the places I visited would be different in summer. I found people outside of the villages to be hostile and suspicious of me. I wear a high visibility jacket when I film so not to get run over and it also makes me look a bit official, this generally means that out with a camera I get left alone. I did feel very conscious of how isolated I was in many of the places and took someone with me when possible. The weather was cold and windy. On one occasion the wind was so strong that I had to have help holding my tripod down. The buffeting wind sound that came from that day added to the bleakness of the final pieces.

SH I grew to like and enjoy the Fens. It's a very misunderstood place as it's not a landscape that is immediately seductive. I would normally be met with a sharp intake of breath upon telling friends I was going to spend considerable time there. I made three trips, each of two to three days, in all the seasons apart from summer. I had snow, sun and everything in between. I made visits to all the science parks in the area but more generally I drove widely throughout the Fens, just exploring.

TNWK The work evolved whilst on long drives, walks and cycles through fen territories in the late winter, early spring. Each time we would try to ask questions that felt like starting points, such as literally to ask people "scuse me, where is 'Silicon Fen'?" and 'does the term 'Silicon Fen' mean any-thing to you?' After each outing our anxiety about having undertaken the commission increased. We were fascinated by the landscape and its histories but unable to make a connection to a workable idea. People we spoke to seemed, in the vast majority, to make no connection with the location 'Silicon Fen' at all. The appearance of the landscape was overwhelmingly rural and bleak. We quickly felt the need to put ourselves in the picture and to perform as researchers. The image that began to develop was that of the hitch-hiker, holding up a sign asking for a lift to 'Silicon Fen'. Precedents in Bob Dylan, Gillian Wearing and Forced Entertainment were all over-familiar to us; but we were also tugging at a sense of being displaced, or rootless, vulnerably located or in transit. Ultimately these images appear in the work with the words digitally erased from our signs presenting an uncertainty about our destination.

Many of those we asked told us confidently that 'Silicon Fen' was in America somewhere. Happily, our visit to the extraordinary Straw Bear Festival in Whittlesey, held in early January, provided a sonic resolution to this confusion. We heard a particular tune being played over and

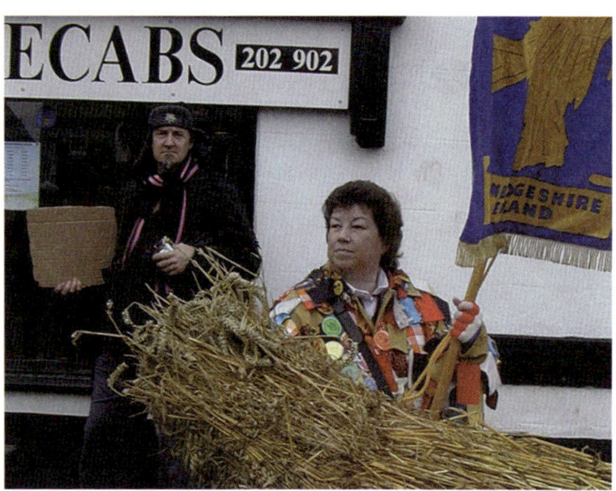

over by precessing bands there; we were curious, recognising it as a quintessentially American song and irretrievably associating it with John Wayne and the ambivalent romance of the frontier. Why was it being played by the Morris Dancers in the middle of the Fens reviving a centuries' old mid-winter communal ritual? Subsequent web research revealed numerous sound files charting the song's progress from a seventeenth century English folk song to American Civil War anthem as depicted in the central movie of John Ford's iconic post-World War Two western trilogy, *She Wore A Yellow Ribbon* (1949). We were struck by the sense of how origin and location become skewed through time, more particularly by this playing back to a notional origin of a pioneering rhetoric that so aptly fitted characterisations of the so-called 'digital frontier'.

SW How do you feel about the exhibition of your work for *Silicon Fen* in the gallery space?

SB The exhibition worked well in the BCA Gallery in Bedford. My original proposal had taken into account the small size of the rooms and the works' relationship with these rooms. I was very pleased with the resulting exhibition. It was all the right size and the sound from the animations was audible in the whole space. BCA were a delight to work with. A small but totally professional gallery, they did everything they had promised; working with them was wonderful.

D+S The exhibition at Peterborough worked as well as it could in that particular space. Although we always had that space in mind we also wanted to create a work which could be shown, effectively in other venues. It was good that the space was painted black, the projections and sound equipment were brilliantly resourced and installed by the *Silicon Fen* team and the technical team at Peterborough. The weaknesses in the installation were more to do with the building than anything else. The entrance and lead-in to the installation was a bit cluttered and multi purpose, which can be distracting and is not the ideal introduction to experience a work. Due to the restricting scale of the space and the limit on where we could house the projectors the projections did not go all the way to the floor which we would have been preferred and there was a door in the space which led off to the next gallery which was also a bit of a distraction, but overall we were pleased with the installation.

AH My aim for the exhibition at King's Lynn was to set up a situation that would allow the viewer to experience a constant shift in physical and cognitive orientation as they moved through the space; from the shifting, flowing perspectives of the film *Cut Drains, Charts, Creeks and Cuts* to clear relationship between viewer, viewpoint and horizon in the large photograph *Blizzard Fen*;

from the horizon-less series of aerial photographs to the physical sensations experienced in front of the cut-outs which, although stripped of much of their detail, create a strong sense of angle or disorientation in the viewer. The scale of the Shakespeare Barn at King's Lynn meant viewers could physically move in and out of the work, viewing it from many different angles and distances. The Babylon Gallery, Ely, is a much smaller space, though, surprisingly, large enough to accommodate all the work from King's Lynn effectively. Babylon's particular interested in new media also made it the perfect place to launch the first phase of howworld.com, which we presented on two laptops in the gallery. The presence of the water outside the door, which bounced flickering light into the gallery enhanced the sense of water being the dominant element in both the work and the world outside.

Howworld is an internet equivalent of a shoebox of forever accumulating stuff. In *Howworld* you can drift, click and zoom your way through different layers and images: mediated graphic, photographic, cartographic and linguistic extracts. *Howworld* is made up of different bits of information gathered during the research phase of making work, but which do not directly become part of the final photographs, installations and animations. In *Howworld* these elements are joined by others, which are integral parts of the artworks. *Howworld* will continue to grow in parallel to other bodies of work. It is a virtual, digital counterpart to ideas that are manifested physically in space, in a space, or of a space.

SC *Fenlandia* has been derived from the location and shown in the region but, due to its online presence, it has been much further afield.

Both versions, the live transmission and the printed still, have something distinct to offer. The colour, revealed by each individual pixel, seems to be evident to a greater degree in the prints. The large format prints expose each individual pixel in the way only a projection or larger screen would be able to match, and the smaller prints concentrate the colour. When lined up together the prints seen sequentially give another sense of time, revealing all sorts of shifts and changes – from the thinning and widening band of night-time throughout the year – to the full moon that *Glenlandia* (the later, Scottish version of the work) has occasionally captured and which appears as a white 'comet' streaking through the night sky but is in fact the moon slipping through the image over time.

The live transmission, by contrast, focuses more on 'the moment' – the 'where is now'. The finding of the moving pixel, the moment that is 'now', can have a sense of personal discovery about it. Unspectacular and modest in scale, each pixel's arrival reveals the hopelessness and the lie in creating this live window to another place, serving to remind us how distant it (the place in the image) really is.

In previous work I have resisted making stills or artefacts from live or installed works as I felt these would only operate as documentation and not stand alone as work in themselves. For me these prints are different – with each image a complete work in itself. It may seem contradictory but I think the reason why they work independently is almost precisely because they don't have the urgency of the 'now' that makes the live work so compelling. They offer a different kind of engagement, more a reflection on time, landscape and observation itself.

TNWK We were commissioned to make a work for the web so its gallery exhibition simply functioned as a signpost to its location on the world wide web. *far from silicon fen* is a work for the web, drawn from the web and designed to be viewed within the context of the web browser interface. One over riding factor for us in responding to the commission was trying to make something that would be workable within reasonable download speed limitations of internet technology widely in public circulation and usage at that time. Remember that broadband was not widely and affordably delivered at that time, so we used stills, sound and text within 'Flash' and built a piece that would take an ordinary net connection speed under 10 minutes to download. With today's technology we could do what we so ardently desired to do at the time, embed digital video.

SW Susan, how did you select the images to print from the hundreds available and decide which to print as A4 and as 150cm?

SC Developing a series over time allows a process of reflection. Whilst all the cameras were interesting in their live iterations, the locations that created the richest, most painterly, durable and diverse range of images were the rural landscapes — in particular *Fenlandia* at the Anchor Inn and *Glenlandia* at Loch Faskally, and it is these that I have focused on in developing a body of printed images from the archives.

There are actually over 4,000 images archived from the original *Fenlandia* at the Anchor Inn alone (the images are saved automatically at 2 hour intervals throughout the year). My aim in selecting images for the exhibition at Babylon Gallery was to show a representative range of stills from across the seasons, at different times of day, in different light and weather conditions. The final choices, once that had been taken into account, were made on aesthetic grounds — which images revealed more information/colour when printed at a large scale, and which worked well in a 'narrative' series.

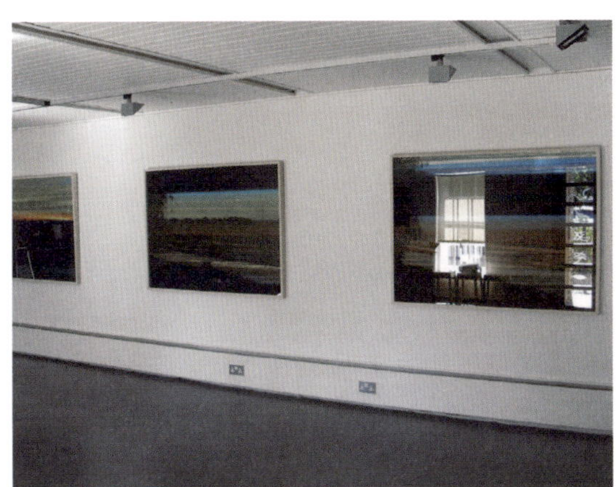

There is a large format print from a *Fenlandia* still captured on 1st January 2005, a thin sliver of a steely grey day with a streak of pink depicting the threshold of daybreak, which when enlarged reveals many individually captured pinks. Each image from the archive when enlarged in this way reveals unseen depths of colour and detail.

SW Has the work produced for *Silicon Fen* been exhibited anywhere else? Does the work relate to other works you have produced since the *Silicon Fen* project?

TNWK Yes, it has been presented for the Interactive Media Studies conference at Miami University, in Oxford, Ohio, at the Cork International Festival of Poetry and Textsounds at Notre Dame University, Illinois. Subsequent works, such *Coleridge's Rime of the Ancient Mariner* built upon our use of gathered audio in *far from silicon fen*. It was TNWK's first substantial collaborative foray into sound composition and, as such, it paved the way for discussions about radio art and so forth that led to initiatives such as Radio Taxi and other work being pursued independently. Also *Throwaway Remarks: Bury is a four letter word* (2005) commissioned by Bury Art Gallery, Greater

Manchester was a text-image public artwork taking over the advertising spaces in all the rubbish bins in the city centre. This work used similar strategies in its generation; walking and talking, the photographic registration of details as noticed and the gathering of portraits initiated through chance conversation and curiosity.

SC As well as the *Silicon Fen* presentations and the *Fenlandia* and *Glenlandia* websites, the work when live and transmitting also exists as a downloadable full screen image which can update live in realtime. This means of transmission has enabled both *Fenlandia* and *Glenlandia* to be exhibited nationally and internationally.

In addition to the solo exhibition at Babylon Gallery, Ely in 2006, *Fenlandia* has been shown in Rhizome ArtBase 101, a netart survey exhibition at the New Museum of Contemporary Art, New York in 2005; The Microwave Media Festival, Hong Kong, 2004; in Data Agency, HTTP Gallery, London and Close Proximity, New Greenham Arts, both organised by SCAN, 2005; The Atrium, South Hill Park 2005; Digital Aesthetic 2, PR1 Gallery, Preston 2006 and Video Vortex, Netherlands Media Art Institute, Amsterdam 2007.

SB The work was extended and exhibited at the Pump House Gallery, London in 2005. Film and Video Umbrella also produced a publication to accompany the work at this venue, which was based on the Ladybird series of books. I am currently applying for funding to make work about the demise of the dawn chorus. This is as a result of what I learnt from making *The Return of the Native*.

Simon Willmoth Your galleries were involved in the *Silicon Fen* project from its early stages of development. Why were you interested in working with Norwich School of Art and Design (Norwich University College of the Arts) and Film and Video Umbrella on the project?

Peterborough Digital Arts *Silicon Fen* was particularly attractive to us as it came at a time when the role of the Art Gallery in Peterborough was developing to become a venue exhibiting, commissioning and promoting digital and new media art.

We had previously worked with FVU on our first digital residency a couple of years before. Norwich School of Art and Design was not only an institution we clearly saw the advantages of working with but who were also prepared to oversee *Silicon Fen* through its development and commissioning stages.

Bedford Creative Arts We knew that FVU had a great reputation, having shown three of their touring pieces. We were keen to increase our regional networks and national profile, to support commissioning in the region, and to secure our position with the Arts Council. We were also attracted by the chance to raise our profile in a different part of the region, to achieve peer group recognition and work with and support other galleries – with a view to future partnership working.

King's Lynn Arts Centre Our involvement with the *Silicon Fen* project seemed a very natural progression, as it was a continuation of an earlier collaborative relationship with Film and Video Umbrella and also reinforced our long-standing connection with Norwich School of Art and Design.

Given our location in West Norfolk, the *Silicon Fen* project brief was perfect, as it reflected upon rural isolation and the way that new technology has opened up instantaneous channels of communication. Being involved with two lead organisations each with an impressive specialism in film, animation and new technologies was extremely beneficial and enabled us to acquire experience and equipment that will be of lasting benefit. The team now have more confidence to work with challenging, cutting-edge technology.

Babylon Gallery The opportunity to work with a network of visual arts organisations, in particular Norwich School of Art and Design and Film and Video Umbrella, as well as the other galleries in the project, came at a very good time: the Babylon Gallery had been open for a couple of years, and had been building a strong local reputation and audiences. We were keen to build regional awareness for the space, at the same time as developing our own skills through the opportunity to work with other commissioning bodies. The particular theme of the commissions also resonated with the developing exhibition policy at Babylon.

SW How did the *Silicon Fen* project and the commission relate to your exhibitions policy and previous exhibitions at the gallery?

BCA BCA Gallery always had a lens-based remit, but having shown a lot of photography, we were keen to show more film work. Animation had been particularly under-represented in our programme. Our exhibitions policy also states a desire to introduce audiences to artists working at a regional, national and international level and this initiative enabled us to do that.

Babylon The programming policy at Babylon related to its location and audience: our core audiences came from a largely rural area, with

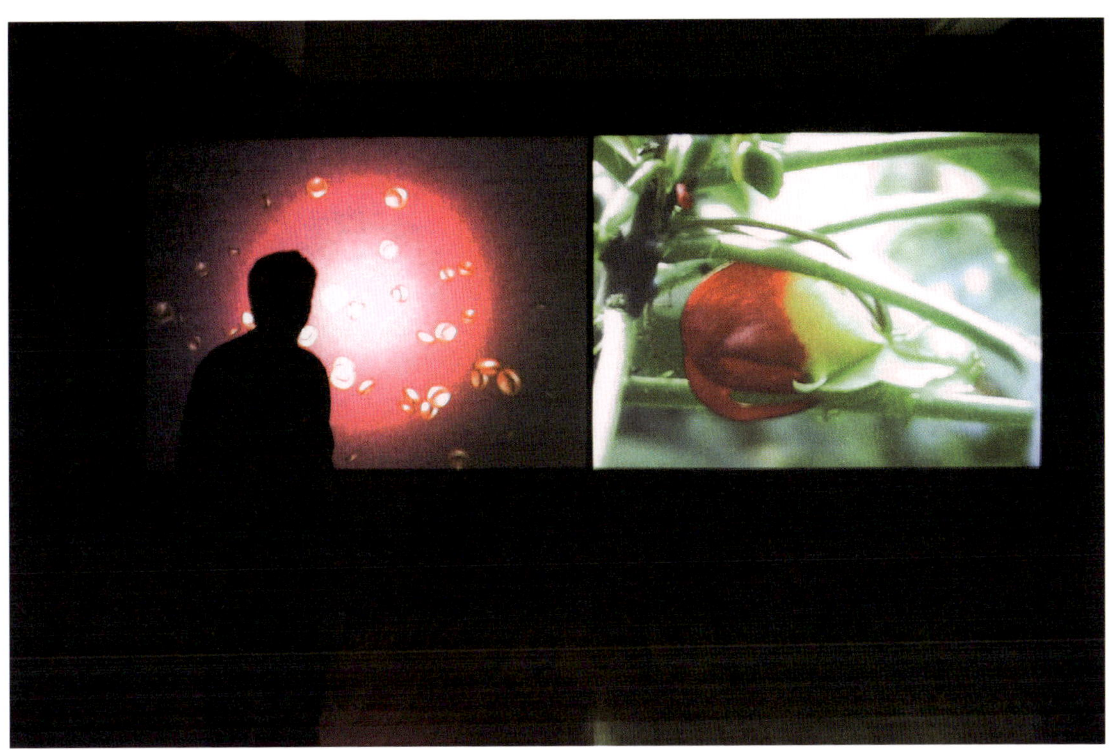

very limited access to public gallery space, and as a publicly funded space we had a responsibility to provide access to a broad range of contemporary visual arts.

When the opportunity to take part in *Silicon Fen* came up, we had recently taken the decision that we should include digital work within our programme and embarked on a pilot programme of four commissions. This programme gave us the opportunity to build on that initial commissioning work.

PDA Our gallery exhibition, Dalziel+Scullion's *Earthdom*, fitted in extremely well with the gallery's exhibition policy, including how the exhibition space was to be used. We are fortunate in having a large and flexible exhibition environment, which we always strive to make use of in as creative way as possible.

KLAC *Silicon Fen* built on previous experience whilst fitting in well with our programming policy to provide a diverse range of work, underpinned by practical educational activities for all ages. Our programme is always balanced to appeal to all audiences through the spectrum from 'art informed' to passers-by and the resulting works were accessible, whilst still utilising new technology and engaging with cutting-edge artistic practice.

SW What was the gallery's experience of exhibiting the commissions – firstly the *Silicon Fen* 'hub' for the three online works, and then the gallery exhibition?

BCA Earlier programming decisions meant that the *Silicon Fen* hub was with us during an exhibition of unrelated, issue based photography as our main show and with hindsight this wasn't the best fit.

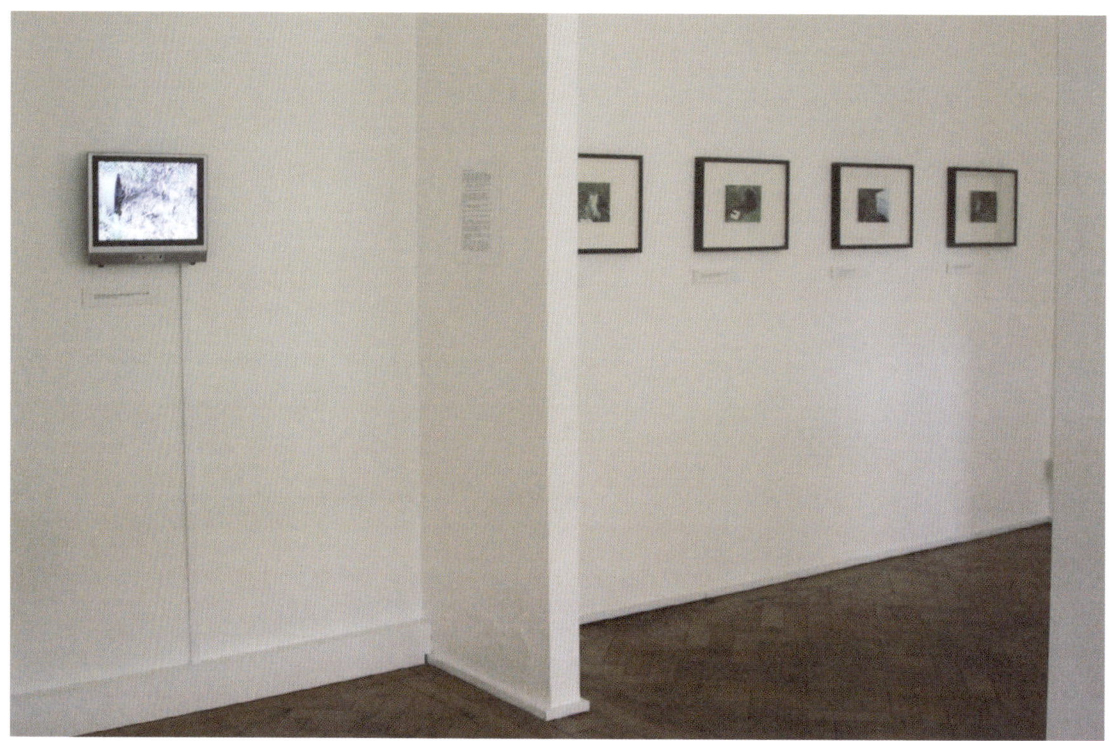

It may have worked better if we had had more time to produce more effective interpretation material to support visitors. Our audiences span all ages and backgrounds and some visitors may be less comfortable with the idea of visiting a gallery to experience online work.

Suky Best's *The Return of the Native*: the development of this body of work enabled a collaboration between the artist and Chris Andrews, the natural history curator of Bedford Museum, which enhanced the relevance of the work for our audiences. Suky Best was an excellent artist to work with, a consummate professional who respected our audience-focused approach. BCA also developed a very positive relationship with the project's technical team who helped ensure we didn't experience any problems with the relatively high quantity of equipment involved in the show.

PDA We were able to 'trail' *Earthdom* by exhibiting the *Silicon Fen* hub during an earlier exhibition. This stand-alone web-based work was popular and effective in itself. *Silicon Fen* provided us with the challenge and the opportunity to exhibit the work in a dramatic form, as *Earthdom* was a double projection video with sound. This invited visitors into an environment we worked hard to make as accessible and thought-provoking as possible.

Babylon Overall, the experience was positive as both commissions sat well within our programme. The particular challenges came around the three-way nature of the project, with the lead commissioning body remote from the Gallery. Therefore, the process of building a relationship with the artist, inherent in previously commissioning carried out directly by the Gallery, was condensed into a much shorter timeframe.

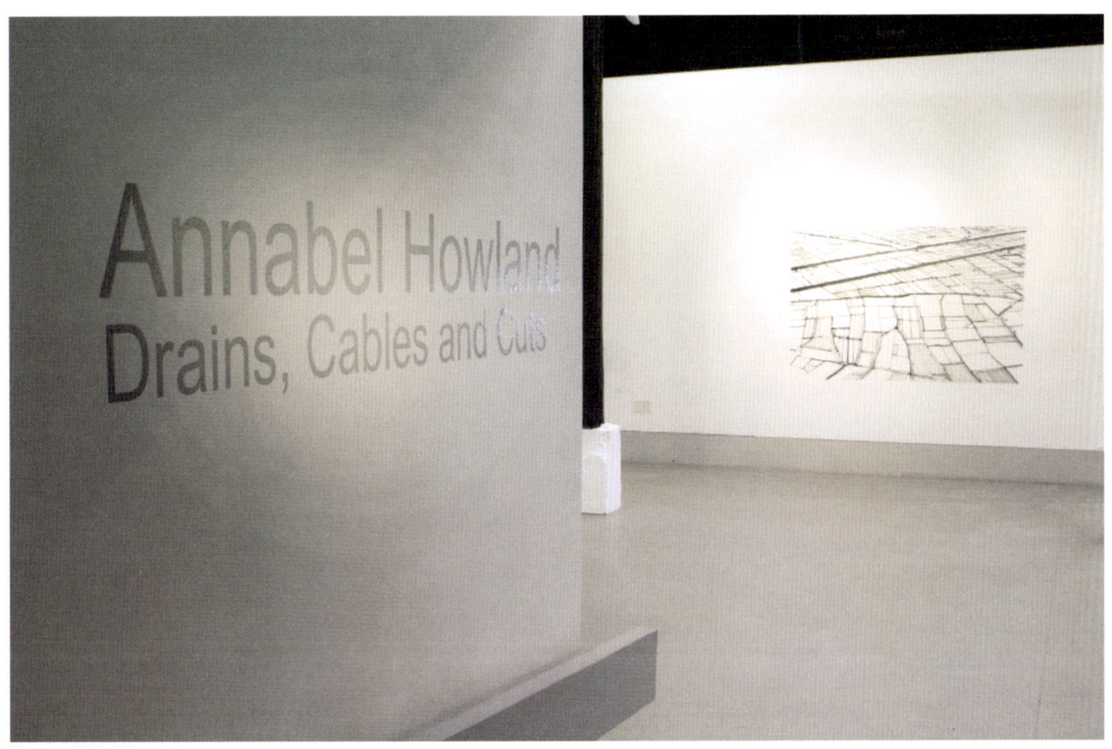

KLAC The first stage of *Silicon Fen* was the commissioned online works shown on the hub. These were displayed via a stand-alone unit sited within the gallery which invited audience participation. The general feedback from the public was that these works were not as engaging as might have been expected, given the excitement of the medium/the idea of artworks on the internet.

Subsequently, the exhibition of Annabel Howland's *Drains, Cables, and Cuts* made far more impact. It was juxtaposed against exhibitions in our other galleries using more traditional media, such as painting and provided an opportunity for some audiences to 'dip their toes' into digital 'waters', as well as attracting new attenders with an interest in new media art. The well researched content was entirely related to the region, so that audiences could access the imagery immediately with a sense of familiarity and those with greater interest could probe further into additional layers of meaning.

The installation of *Drains, Cables, and Cuts* was labour-intensive and painstaking, but the results were breathtaking. The artist worked closely with staff who took the utmost care to display the thin, fragile framework of the dissected photographs and the lofty space within the newly refurbished Shakespeare Barn was an ideal venue for Annabel Howland's meticulous work.

SW What was the public's response to the exhibitions in your galleries?

PDA We always try to provide a varied visitor experience and *Earthdom* was no exception. The way in which *Earthdom* was exhibited, sound and imagery in a space darkened to

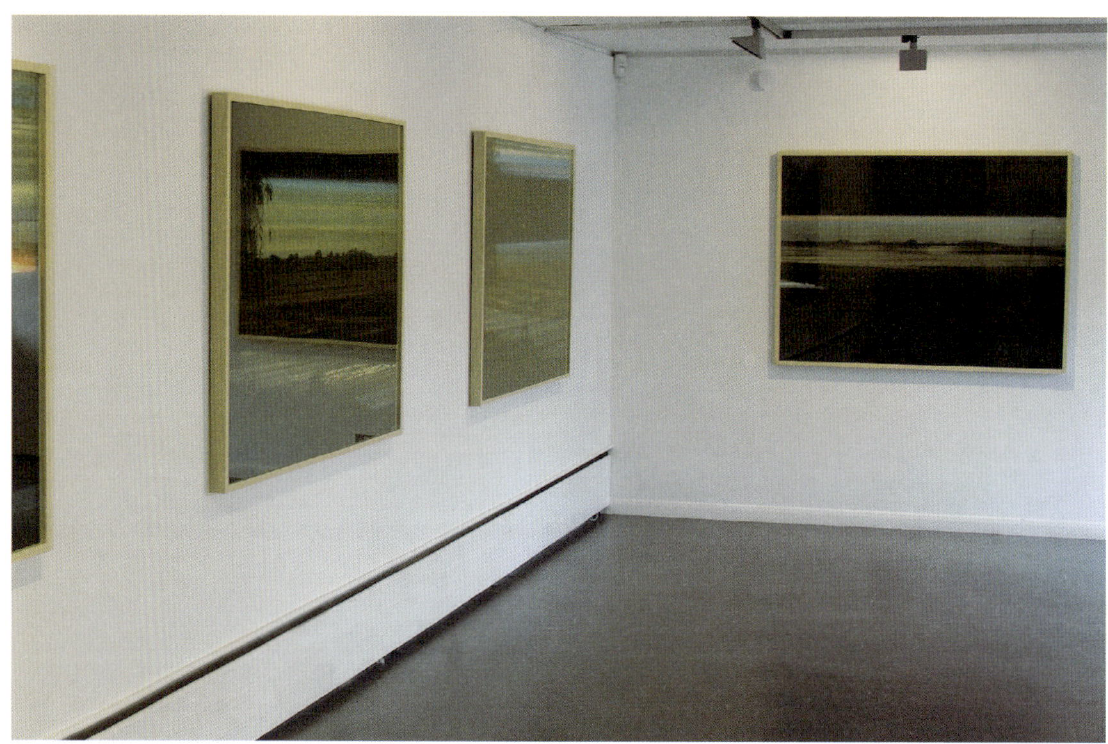

highlight the experience, caused more than one comment on the contemplative nature of engaging with the work.

Babylon Audience reactions varied widely, which is what we expect for commissions working in a digital medium. The audience for exhibitions at the Gallery was very diverse, including people for whom the *Silicon Fen* exhibitions were their first or only experience of work in a digital medium. However, the content of the work and the combination of still images with the screen-based work enabled most people to find a positive experience. The overall themes of *Silicon Fen* encouraged people to reflect upon and reconsider the landscape around them.

Responses to Annabel Howland's *Howworld* website tended to vary according to age: younger visitors were comfortable to explore and experiment, older people needed specific encouragement to engage with the work on the website. Susan Collins' *Fenlandia* drew specific comments about the relationship with time.

BCA From the hub, Susan Collins' work was well received by our audiences as they felt it exploited the online medium most effectively, whereas some people felt that they would prefer to see Stephen Hughes' work in a more traditional physical exhibition.

We had a fantastic response to Suky Best's work in the gallery. Visitors told us they found it moving, accessible and thoughtful, and the local links and environmental focus were important. The work gave a gentle introduction to animation and new technology for some visitors. We had over 100 visitors to the private view and 1,028 visits

Susan Collins *Fenlandia*
Babylon Gallery September-November 2006

during the six-week exhibition. 64% of visitors rated the show as 'excellent' and a further 32% as 'good'.

SW Has there been any further outcome for the gallery as a result of working on the *Silicon Fen* project?

Babylon Working on the *Silicon Fen* project gave us the time and opportunity to develop thinking around the relationship between the Gallery and its context, building on the commissioning we had already done, and feeding in to the next phase of development. Working particularly with commissions that had focused on the specificity of the landscape, added an additional dimension to our understanding of contextually-based practice. The Babylon Gallery was on the water-side in Ely, with windows from the exhibition space looking out on to the river and the fen landscape beyond: these two commissions high-lighted the relationship with the physical space beyond the gallery.

BCA We have cemented our reputation with FVU, which may lead to co-commissioning in the future. Through Suky Best we have generated a network of influential artist advocates who have written letters of support for Arts Council bids and recommended us to other practitioners. The very positive feedback we received from the artist has given us more confidence in our own professionalism, knowing we are able to respond to the needs of more established artists. Promotion of the exhibition to local conservation bodies led directly to the cultivation of a new trustee for BCA from the RSPB.

As a result of our involvement in *Silicon Fen*, we were also invited to become part of *Accession*, another partnership between four regional galleries, which this time involved international residencies. We have stronger links with the other *Silicon Fen* galleries and with the Pump House Gallery in Battersea who staged an exhibition of a further development of *The Return of the Native* after us. The new equipment has been used to enhance our ability to show more moving image work and will be appreciated by the artists who come to participate in our new residency programme. The sale of some of Suky Best's work to the Open University has encouraged us to become part of the Arts Council's *Buy Art* scheme and to develop our selling skills.

The biggest success for BCA Gallery was the selection of the right artist, and the fact that she worked directly with us during the creation of her body of work. With this in mind, we'd like to acknowledge the key role played by Sarah Blomfield, Director of BCA at the time of the original selection.

KLAC It is always a privilege to work with other organisations and to learn from their experience. The team at King's Lynn Arts Centre have a greater appreciation of the rigours of exhibiting works involving new technology and a commitment to continue to show this kind of work.

PDA *Silicon Fen* provided us with the opportunity to make links with other galleries, organisations and institutions. It enabled us to experience how other galleries engaged in the same project albeit with very different work.

One of the most important elements of *Silicon Fen* for us was being part of a much bigger, regional project and this is an experience we would hope to repeat.

Artists' Biographies

Suky Best
Born – London, 1962
Lives and works – London

Selected solo exhibitions since 2001
2008 *Rodeo* (with Rory Hamilton) Danielle Arnaud Contemporary Art, London
2007 *About Running* Baltic, Gateshead
      From the Archive UCLH, NHS Trust, London
      Stone Voices Sculpture in Woodland, Co Wicklow, Ireland
2005 *Return of the Native* BCA Gallery, Bedford; Pump House Gallery, London
      Wild West (with Rory Hamilton), Danielle Arnaud Contemporary Art, London
      Recent Work Danielle Arnaud Contemporary Art, London
2001 *10 Journeys Dartmoor* Insight/Aha/Da2 Commision and touring
      the way we live now Lighthouse Media Gallery, Wolverhampton

Selected Group exhibitions since 2001
2007 *Berwick Film and Media Festival* various venues Berwick-on-Tweed
      Towards a New Ease Fotomuseum, Winterthur, Switzerland
      Close at Hand Contemporary Art Projects, London
      Scodown! D.U.M.B.O. Arts Centre, New York
      Bloomberg Art Futures Bloomberg Space, London
      Visual Fictions Fenton Gallery, Cork, Ireland
2006 *Tulca* Festival of Visual Art, Galway
      Naturaleza:Photoespania 2006 Various Venues, Madrid
      Timeless:time, landscape and new media Harbourfront Centre, Toronto
      MIMA:offsite Institute of Modern Art, Middlesbrough
      His Life is Full of Miracles Site Gallery, Sheffield
      Video Art & Drawing, Art Projects London Art Fair, London
      The Lightbox Tate Britain, London
      The Projection Room County Hall, Dun Laoghaire, Eire
      Art Futures 2005 Bloomburg Space, London
2004 *Magic within Reason* Domo Ball Gallery, London
      Trace edition Hirschl Contemporary Art, London
      Exhumed The Museum of Garden History, London
2002 *Winners Exhibition John Kobul 10 Anniversary* National Portrait Gallery, London
      Julian Walker and Suky Best Unit 2, London

Awards/Other Projects
2007-08 *Early Birds* Animate! and Channel 4
2007 *From the Archive* Commission at University College Hospital, London
      About Running Great North Run, Moving Image Commission
      Stone Voices Sculpture in Woodland Commission, Devil's Glen, Ireland
      Horses Permanent Animation for Octav Boctar Wing, Great Ormond St
        NHS Hospital, London
2004-05 *Wellcome Trust* SCIART Research and Development Award
2002 *London Arts Board* individual artist award

Susan Collins www.susan-collins.net/fenlandia
Born – London, 1964
Lives and works – London

Selected solo exhibitions since 2001
2006 *Fenlandia* Babylon Gallery, Ely
2002 *Transporting Skies* Site Gallery Sheffield and Newlyn Art Gallery Penzance
2001 *In Conversation* British Council, Hackescher Markt, Berlin

Selected Group exhibitions since 2001
2008 *Slow Fields* Susan Collins and Tim Head, Osterwalders Art Office, Hamburg
      Travelogue One in The Other Gallery, London
      Work and Play Terrace Gallery, Harewood House, Leeds

2007	*Multiplicities* ARC Projects, Sofia, Bulgaria
	Video Vortex Netherlands Media Art Institute/Montevideo, Amsterdam
	Webspace Vestsjĺllands Kunstmuseum, SŅro, Denmark
	Outlook Express(ed) Oakville Galleries, Ontario
	Digital Aesthetic 2, Harris Museum and Art Gallery, Preston
2006	*A Retrospective of British Media Art* Kunsthaus, Dresden
	Timeless York Quay Art Centre, Toronto
	REMOTE Plimsoll Gallery, Hobart, Tasmania
2005	*Blur of the Otherworldly* Center for Art and Visual Culture, UMBC, Baltimore
	StoryRooms Museum of Science and Industry, Manchester
	Rhizome ArtBase 101 New Museum of Contemporary Art, NYC
2004	*Haunted Media* Site Gallery, Sheffield
2003	*@rt Outsiders – Space Art* Maison Européenne de la Photographie, Paris

Awards/Other Projects

2007	*Garry B Fritz Imagemaker Award for Excellence* SPE, Miami
2005	*Underglow* commission for Light Up Queen Street, Corporation of London
	Glenlandia commissioned for Threshold Artspace by Horsecross, Perth
2002	*Tate in Space* commissioned for Tate Online and nominated for a BAFTA interactive in 2004
2001	*Royal Society of Arts Art for Architecture Award* for collaboration with architect Sarah Wigglesworth on a Classroom of the Future for Mossbrook Special School, Sheffield (completed 2005)

Dalziel+Scullion www.dalzielscullion.com
Matthew Dalziel, Born – Irving, Scotland, 1957
Louise Scullion, Born – Helensburgh, Scotland, 1966
Live and work – Dundee, Scotland

Selected solo exhibitions since 2001

2008	*The Earth Turned To Bring Us Closer* Feinstein Lighthouse, Norway as part of *On The Edge* project for Stavanger 2008
2007	*More Than Us* Great Glen House, Scottish Natural Heritage, Inverness, Scotland
	Source An Tobar, Isle of Mull, Scotland
	Some Distance From the Sun Aberdeen Art Gallery & Museum, Scotland
2006	*The Earth Turned To Bring Us Closer* Kelvingrove Art Gallery & Museum, Glasgow
2005	*Breath taking* various UK billboards, Deveronarts UK
	Earthdom Peterborough Digital Arts
2004	*Genus* Aberystwyth Arts Centre
2003	*Storm* Gallery of Modern Art, Glasgow
	Genus National Museum of Photography, Film and Television, Bradford
	Applied Metaphysics pt 2 Catalyst Arts, Belfast
	Dalziel+Scullion Taigh Chearsabhagh, Lochmaddy, North Uist, Western Isles
	Home Manchester City Art Gallery, Manchester
	Water Falls Down Ibid Projects, Vilnius, Lithuania
2002	*Raptor* Houldsworth, London
	Aura A Houldsworth, London
	Home Milton Keynes Art Gallery
2001	*Home* Fruitmarket Gallery, Edinburgh
	Meltwater Sadler's Wells Theatre, London

Selected Group exhibitions since 2001

2008	*One Minute* with composer Craig Armstrong, *Festival De St Denis* Paris, France
	Transitional State Forest Hall, Edinburgh Arts Festival Scotland
	On Edge Travellinggallery, Edinburgh Arts Festival Scotland
	Scottish Contemporary Art From Glasgow Museums Limerick City Gallery of Art, Ireland
	Artes Mundi Prize The National Galleries of Wales, Cardiff, Wales

2007   *Grey Alder* JICPB Cube Gallery: Jarnac, France; Cairo, Egypt; Portree, Scotland (2008)
            Inchinomiya, Japan; BNvlingbjerg, Denmark
        Digital VD Philadelphia, Kyoto, Japan; Dundee, Scotland; Leiden, Netherlands;
            New York; Warsaw, Poland
2006   *Northern City* The Lighthouse, Glasgow, Scotland
2005   *Creative Futures* Crawford Arts Centre, St Andrew's, Scotland
        Freeze Frame Stephen Lawrence Gallery, London
2004   *Blind Sight* Titanik Galleria, Turku, Finland; Centre Space VRC,
            Dundee Contemporary Arts, Scotland
        Forest Wolverhampton Art Gallery, England
2003   *Hot Summer in the City* Sean Kelly Gallery, New York
        Science, poetry, and art Dundee Contemporary Arts, Dundee, Scotland
        A Great Piece of Turf Danielle Arnaud Gallery, London
        Frozen Site Gallery, Sheffield, England
2002   *Living Landscape* West Cork Arts Centre, Ireland; An Tuireann Arts Centre,
            Isle of Skye, Scotland
        First International Biennal of Video Art Centre of Contemporary Art, Tel Aviv, Israel
        My Father is the Wise Man of the Village Fruitmarket Gallery, Edinburgh
        Target Art Madison Square Park, New York
2001   *New Visions of the Sea* National Maritime Museum, London
        Water Falls Down Edinburgh International Film Festival Scotland
        Here and Now McManus Gallery, Dundee Contemporary Arts, Generator
            and Aberdeen Art Gallery, Scotland
        Shriek From an Invisible Box Merguro Museum of Art, Tokyo, Japan
        Re-mote Photographer's Gallery, London
        Living the Land Duff House, Banff, Scotland

Awards/Other Projects
2008   Short listed for the international *Artes Mundi Prize*
2007   *The Saltire Award for Art in Architecture*
2005   *The Eco Prize For Creativity*
        Creative Scotland Award
        The Saltire Award for Art in Architecture
2004   *Royal Incorporation of Architects Scotland* Creativity Award
        Henry Moore Foundation Award
2002-03 *Fellowship* Museum of Photography, Film and Television, Bradford
2002   *Carnegie Award*
        PESCA Award
2001   *Scottish Arts Council* (Major Bursary) Visual Artists Award

Annabel Howland www.annabelhowland.nl
Born – Bishop's Stortford, England, 1967
Lives and works – Amsterdam, Netherlands

Selected solo exhibitions since 2001
2006   *Drains, Cables, and Cuts – Silicon Fen*, King's Lynn Arts Centre and
            Babylon Gallery, Ely, England
2004   *Stay* Futura, Prague, Czech Republic
2003   *Lines of Disposition. Lines of Site.* Archipel, Apeldoorn, Netherlands
        Expanding Cuts TENT's Curve, Rotterdam Photo Biennial, Netherlands
2002   *Cut Land/Terre Tranchée (+ residency)*, Centre VU, Québec, Canada

Selected Group exhibitions since 2001
2008   *There is No Road* LABoral, Gijón, Spain
2004   *Tracer.* Paraeducation Department, (Annie Fletcher and Sarah Pierce)
            Witte de with Center for Contemporary Art, Rotterdam, Netherlands
2002   *Perspective 2002* Ormeau Baths Gallery, Belfast, Northern Ireland
2001   *Landscape Trauma in the Age of Scopophilia* The Gallery, London;
            Leeds Metropolitan University Gallery. Curated by Richard Hylton

Awards/Other Projects

2006- *Howworld* www.howworld.com funded by Fonds BKVB
2004 *Perspectives* St Lucas Andreas Hospital, Amsterdam, Netherlands
Trebesice Tracks Castle Trebesice, Bohemia, Czech Republic
West St Lucas Andreas Hospital, Amsterdam, Netherlands

Stephen Hughes
Born – Brighton, England, 1968
Lives and works – Brighton, England

Selected solo exhibitions since 2001

2005 *Stephen Hughes: New Work* Open Eye Gallery, Liverpool
Robert Mann Gallery New York
2004 *Stephen Hughes* Galerie Thomas Zander, Cologne, Germany
2003 *Blue Sky Gallery* Oregon Center for the Photographic Arts, Portland
Art Köln Foerderkoje Galerie Thomas Zander, Cologne, Germany
2002 *Stephen Hughes Photographs* Galerie Pole Image Haute Normandie,
Rouen, France
2001 *Stephen Hughes Photographs* De La Warr Pavilion, Bexhill on Sea, England

Selected Group exhibitions since 2001

2007 *From Where you Stand*, IPG, Battle, England
Alone Together POC, La Halles, Pont-en-Royan, France
2006 *From Brighton* Diaphane, La Grange, Montreuil-sur-Breche, France
Alone Together POC, Galerie Nouvelles Images, Den Haag, Netherlands
2004 *Forum fur Photographie* POC, Cologne, Germany
2004 *Vagues 2* Museum Malraux, Le Havre, France

Awards/Other Projects

2004 *Arts Council England and University of Sunderland International Research
Fellow* University of Santiago de Compostela, Spain
2004 *Artist In Residence* Lightworks, Syracuse
2003 *Art Köln Foerderkoje* Galerie Thomas Zander, Cologne, Germany
2003 British Council grant to artists scheme

TNWK www.thingsnotworthkeeping.com
Cris Cheek, Born – London, 1955
Lives and works – Oxford, Ohio, USA
Kirsten Lavers, Born – Redhill, England, 1961
Lives and works – Cambridge, England

Selected solo exhibitions since 2001

2003 *'we are taking these steps because words must mean what they
say jack straw'* Dartington Gallery, Totnes, Devon
2001 *end of the line* Platform, London

Selected Group exhibitions since 2001

2007 *Once Upon a Time in the Best Western* Miami Art Gallery, Oxford Ohio
2006 *Coleridge's Rime of the Ancient Mariner*, Kettles Yard Open, Cambridge, England
2005 *Retrospective Scree(n)d* Text Festival, Bury, England
2004 *wardrawing* in *Flotation*, Wysing Arts and Cambourne Business Park,
Cambridgeshire, England
2003 *Total Writing London* Camden People's Theatre, London

Awards/Other Projects

2005 *Throwaway Remarks – Bury is a four letter word* Cultural Quarter
Temporary Commission, Text Festival, Bury, England
2007 *Sheet of Paper* part of *The Disappearance of Latitude: Live Presence and
Realtime in Contemporary Practice*, Chicago School of Art
2002-06 *The Books* – a subscription graphic novel series.
1999-01 *Millennium Collection*

Edited by Simon Willmoth and Steven Bode
Designed by Richard Bonner-Morgan
Printed by David Holyday at Apollo Limited

Printed in an edition of 500
ISBN 978-1-904270-27-0
©2008 Film and Video Umbrella, the artists and the authors

Film and Video Umbrella 8 Vine Yard London SE1 1QL
T 020 7407 7755 F 020 7407 7766 E info@fvu.co.uk

Elements of the Susan Collins' interview text have been adapted
from interviews with Carlo Zanni in Magazine électronique du
CIAC No 25 – été 2006 and Sean Cubitt, publication pending.

This publication is dedicated to the memory of Peter Buckland

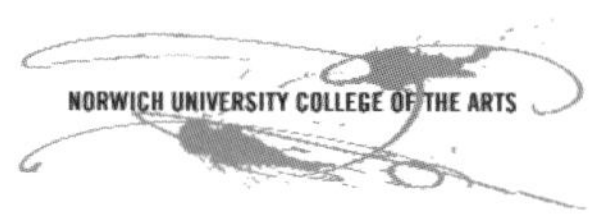
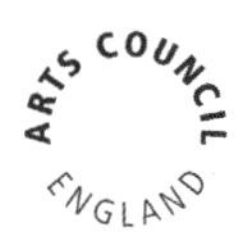
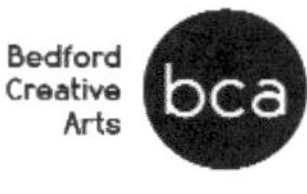
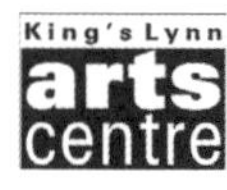
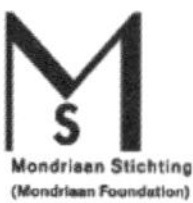
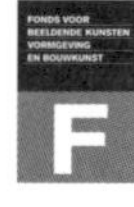